LIFE LESSONS

EVERYTHING
YOU EVER WISHED YOU HAD LEARNED
IN KINDERGARTEN

BY
DONNALYNN CIVELLO

Dedication

To Heidger Marx

For being my greatest teacher in this life.
Thank you for being part of my journey.

Contents

Contents

Contents

Introduction

Nobody ever said life was going to be easy, but then again, no one ever prepared us for it either. At age five we begin school - kindergarten through University - where we are expected to learn intellectually through mental constructs. As life goes on, we find that the real learning happens through life experience in which we learn the wisdom of our actions and the consequences of them. They say that is something you can never teach. I disagree with that.

Life doesn't have to be difficult; we are the ones who complicate it for ourselves. We are all here to learn certain life lessons – lessons we have chosen for ourselves. Wouldn't it be easier if we were told that information upfront? Wouldn't it be easier if we were told, "Hey, remember you are here to learn self-esteem. Throughout your life, you are going to attract people who are going to take advantage of you, take you for granted, make you feel not worthy. When this happens, don't feed the lesson; face it, overcome it and make your life better because of it. When you get the lesson, it stops." Why don't they tell us that in kindergarten?

Life lessons are not complicated; they are actually very easy, but when we don't get the lesson, the lesson repeats, which is extremely arduous and painful. These lessons are extremely simple concepts but extremely powerful in their healing ability. Had we learned these concepts early in life, we would all be much more consciously aware of our lives as adults.

My role is to help people find their life lessons and address them so they can move on with their lives. That is my work, but it wasn't always that way…

I never set out to be a life coach or anything close, but life clearly had other plans for me. I should start out by saying that I am a New Yorker, through and through. I am also a classic over-achiever (guess that is pretty much the same thing!). I collect degrees, maybe because I've always been under the impression that they were necessary and that they somehow determined how intelligent and successful one would be in life. Wow, was I wrong! I have since learned that education is extremely limited in its ability to teach us about life. Conversely, I have learned that experience is our greatest teacher. And when life's experiences beckon, it's time for that life-altering wake-up call. I know, because I got mine six years ago.

In 2009, I had it all. It was almost as if my life were sourced out of a page of New York Magazine. I was stylish, social, an advertising/publishing executive and a designer. I had my MBA and was a graduate student of interior design working as a Creative Services Director at a national design magazine. I was living on Madison Avenue directly across from the Metropolitan Museum of Art and Central Park, spending summers in Fire Island and the Hamptons, traveling to Europe for long weekends and holidays and enjoying the hottest new restaurants, champagne brunches and parties with my Euro friends.

I had also just moved in with the man of my dreams whom I believed I was marrying. He was two years older, European, 6'6" and extremely good looking with piercing blue eyes that could look right through you. He was a perfect gentleman; always opening doors for me and pulling back seat chairs. I always thanked him for every small gesture of kindness and attentiveness he gave me because they made me feel safe and loved. He was a beautiful man; a kind soul, extremely refined with high social graces and good manners. He was highly intelligent; he had a PhD in organic chemistry and had a great job in high tech. He was very charming and always drew people to him with his beautiful, warm smile. His energy was magnetic. He was so knowledgeable about everything – very much on top of all current events – in any part of the world. He also had the most impressive love of history and could recite any historical event and the impact it had on today's modern world. Even more impressive, he could discuss the politics and socio-economic standing of any country. To me, he was a walking encyclopedia of knowledge and not a day went by that I wasn't impressed with him. I always told him that he was amazing. That used to upset him because he never wanted to be put on a pedestal.

He balanced me. I know I am very intelligent, but my knowledge is much more emotional and grounded in wisdom and spirit. Even though I am an MBA, read like a fiend and am very up to date with current events and such, I felt like he grounded me because he was very good in dealing with the material world (finances, taxes, investing, real estate; all things that don't really interest me). For him, I brought to the table a new perspective on life; a higher spiritual perspective that he hadn't thought about and a real emotional intelligence that he was impressed and inspired by. He wanted that wisdom and used to ask many questions about it. We were able to share our lives and our gifts with each other and grow with/learn from each other. It was a perfect union for us.

We were also very social; we had lots of friends and did the New York City thing –parties, restaurants and exploring new areas of the city on our "weekend journeys" together. We loved getting lost in random neighborhoods of Brooklyn, Bronx or Lower East Side taking in the micro-cultures and documenting it through photography (one of his passions). We also liked to escape by taking weekend trips out of town to go hiking or to the ocean. We both loved walking by the ocean and promised ourselves we would one day move to California. We both have a passion for travel and took many trips together; many to Europe to visit with friends and family. We also had a summer home with friends in Fire Island. Basically, we spent all of our time together but our happiest times were spent on a weekend afternoon as "bed slugs"; cuddling in bed and talking/laughing for hours about anything and everything while taking intermittent catnaps in each other's arms. We connected on such a deep level through our interests and our yearning to know one another. We would joke that if we talked on the phone, four hours would pass before we even blinked an eye. Who talks for four hours? This was my perfect relationship and it matched my correspondingly perfect life.

Well, little did I know that my seemingly perfect life was about to unravel right before my eyes. They say that *in life you don't get dealt any hand that you're not able to play.* I am glad that someone up there thought I was ready to play this one because at the time, I wasn't so sure.

Let me start by saying that *life can change on a dime, and it usually does.* I moved in with my boyfriend to start a new life on March 1st of 2009. On March 15th, just two short weeks later, I went in to work on a Monday morning to find out that the magazine I worked for had closed its doors overnight. Clearly, I had missed the late night memo that had gone out. Within a couple months, this man who was my world, the love of my life and the one I thought I was marrying left me for another woman whom I had met at an Oktoberfest party two weeks earlier. She was really beautiful, really sweet, and really smart... I guess I should have seen that coming, but I didn't. Nor did he. He worked at the same company with her, never really interacting, but knew of each other. That afternoon, he very impulsively decided to pursue her for two weeks behind my back, then chose to be with her. Shocked and heartbroken, I then faced the harsh reality of losing my home that we shared together – a beautiful, pre-war-style apartment on Madison Avenue across from the MET and Central Park. Devastated, it was all I could do to just catch my breath and think, "What just happened?"

As a reminder, back in 2009, our country (and most of Europe) was in the throes of recession, and many were out of work. And here I was unemployed, homeless and completely heartbroken. To add insult to injury, (*because that's how life works; when it rains, it pours*) I had limited resources - $98 in my bank account to be exact. Unfortunately, I wasn't very good at saving. My Diane Von Furstenberg dresses were more important to me and I had a fetish for Furla handbags, which didn't help matters any! Obviously not having any money is never a good equation for successful life in New York City.

I was fortunate enough to be able to sleep on friends' sofas for three months while trying to put the pieces back together. All the while I kept thinking, "Why did this happen to me? What am I meant to learn from it and how can I put the pieces back together again in a way that will make me better?" This was my turning point. I should back up and tell you that to date I have been schooled in over 20 years of spiritual study and I knew (even at that time) that I wasn't the victim here. I knew I had that choice – the choice as to whether I was the *victim or the master of my life*. I just needed to figure out how that mastery was going to work! This was an integral part of my path – *learning how to rebuild after the destruction*. And, let's face it, I had all the time in the world, with nowhere to go, nothing to do and no money to do it with. All I could do was sit and stare at myself in the mirror and say, "OK, what next?"

I knew I wasn't going to figure out everything overnight. After all, Rome wasn't built in a day. I knew enough to realize that *life is a puzzle – one where the pieces come together slowly*.

Well, it was definitely time to start putting the pieces back together… one step in front of the other. They say *baby steps to happiness*. They couldn't be more right. During those very difficult months, the only responsibility I had was to teach three yoga classes per week. I had always taught yoga on the side, never really thinking it could be a viable full-time career. I enjoyed teaching and inspiring my students by giving them little bits of "wisdom for living" each week – wisdom that I learned from my spiritual teachers and from all my years of spiritual study.

After my personal breakdown, I realized that I had an even greater responsibility to share my growth and insights with these beautiful students in hopes that they might learn something from my difficult plight. What started out as a cathartic healing for myself had turned into a shared journey into learning how to overcome life's challenges. At every class, I would sit down in front of my students and tell them what I had learned about life that week. As a result, my talks became much more personal, relatable and less esoteric. Those classes changed me on a cellular level and I realized that all the spiritual teachings in the world can't help you if they can't direct you inwards and give you the tools you need to deal with your own personal crises.

Introduction

And so my new role in life began and a whole new career in life coaching and spiritual counseling would soon start unfolding in front of me. Students would come up to me after class and thank me for my words of wisdom and inspiration. They would tell me that it was just what they needed to hear at that moment. They would then ask me if I could email them my essay so they could send it onto a friend who needed to hear that same inspiration. I never had it written down unfortunately. My talks were always just in my head until a year later, 2010, when I decided to start capturing those thoughts and keep them in an online journal so students could quickly access them if they needed inspiration. That online journal became Ethereal Wellness, my blog (etherealwellness.wordpress.com). It took on a life of its own and has been picked up (at the time of this publication) in over 92 countries.

I started out casually counseling my yoga students on their life troubles after class, sometimes meeting them at a vegan café or Starbucks for a chat. I found that they needed support, inspiration and, most importantly, they needed to learn how to reframe their situations so they could see the lesson and begin to move beyond it. I would tell these students that *nothing is as it appears to be* – that all the situations in our lives are only happening for us to learn something from them. It is in that learning that we as souls evolve and can create better life situations for ourselves moving forward. This always seemed to resonate with them and together we would draw up a plan for how they would work through this lesson and make their life better because of it.

Life is funny - d*estiny has a way of finding you*. I know this to be true; I have lived it myself. In fact, I tell my clients that the seeds of the work you are here to do can always be found in your interests. Looking back, I should have taken my own advice. In whatever office setting I was at – Ogilvy & Mather, Saatchi & Saatchi, Grey Advertising, Interbrand or Clodagh Design - I was ALWAYS the office psychologist. Colleagues (and even bosses) would always somehow end up in front of me telling me their work-related problems or relationship issues. I genuinely enjoyed helping them and giving them the inspiration and support they needed to handle their situations. For a brief moment in time, I actually thought about getting a PhD in psychotherapy, but after realizing how long it would take I quickly decided against it!

Flash forward to today: with several trainings under my belt (some things never change!) in Intuitive Counseling/Life Coaching, Pranic Healing Psychotherapy, Holistic Health Coaching and Ayurvedic Nutrition, I work with clients every day to help them live healthier and happier lives. I teach them how to identify their *life lessons* and *life purpose* as it was taught to me and, more importantly, we discuss how those life lessons manifest as patterns in their daily lives. I explain to clients all the time that the longer it takes you to get these lessons, the harder they get. So get them now! After all, our work in life is to *get the lesson and get out* so you can move forward with your life and not stay stuck in repetitive patterns.

So I offer this book to you as my gift. *Life Lessons* is genuinely everything you wished you had learned in kindergarten. It's a compilation of many of the life lessons that I have personally garnered along my journey and those I have learned through my 20+ years of spiritual study with several prominent spiritual teachers (whom I prefer to keep private). It is a modest book of essays taken directly from my blog and some of the inspiration behind them. I hope it gives you a bit of support and new insight into the situations in your own life.

I do want to leave you with this last thought; looking back, I have to say that the very dark time in my life, as difficult as it was for me, made me BETTER. It made me a better teacher, a better coach/counselor, a better friend, a better colleague, a better partner, a better person and it set me on a much better path in my life. I wouldn't have traded that experience for the world. It made me who I am today. It taught me many of the most important life lessons that are out there. And if only we could realize that the happy times in our lives are just the rewards, and that *the most rewarding times are actually the difficult times* (because those are the periods when we do the most growth and learning), then we would be able to look at those situations differently. If I knew then what I know now, I wouldn't have let myself get so caught up in the drama of day-to-day. I would have learned to smile and say, "OK, universe, bring it! I am ready for whatever you are dishing out." After all, *life is just a game. It doesn't matter whether you win or lose; it only matters how you play it.* How have you been playing your life? Are you ready to arm yourself with better tools? This book should give you just that. I wish you all the best on your personal journey. Stay in touch with me; I would love to hear about your life lessons and how they have changed your life – dcivello@ethereal-wellness.com.

In gratitude,
Donnalynn

Be Who You Are

Don't try and be someone else. It never works.
Try being yourself; it's the ONLY person you can be.

Knowing who you are is half the battle in life.
If you do not know who you are,
how can you negotiate your way through your life?
This is where your journey begins.

Life is a process of learning about yourself -
Learning about how special and unique you are -
Allowing yourself to be who you are and
not trying to change yourself for anyone else.

If who you are doesn't work for someone,
then that person doesn't work in your life.
Be who you are.

Why would you want to be anyone else?

Chapter 1

Be Who You Are

I was always someone who cared too much about what people thought of me. I always wanted to be accepted. I always had to be part of the "in crowd" at school.

But even though I wanted to be accepted, I liked the idea that I could be myself and be an independent person not subject to the rules or dictates of others. So even though I was always part of the "in crowd", I was always on the periphery; accepted as an integral part of the group, but never the main attraction. I kept my distance and my privacy. That has always been my modus operandi. And to this day, I still uphold it.

As independent as I am, I can tell you that the yoga and wellness community in NYC is a tight one that definitely brings up everyone's need for approval and acceptance. It can breed many cliques, believe it or not! I can say with all honesty that I adore all my fellow teachers, I support them and I enjoy spending time with them. I have successfully resisted being classified as part of any clique. Why, you might ask? Because I am proud of who I have become, I like who I am and I think who I am can stand alone. It took me 30 years to realize this. I am someone who is accepted and respected in my community for the work I do and for the relationships I foster, and that alone is more than enough.

Today, I consider myself to be a teacher, and teachers lead; they never follow. And in my humble opinion, real teachers never have a need for followers. It's the follower who needs the teachings. Teachers always stand on their own, apart from the crowd. I teach my clients/yoga students the foundation which is to always be who they are and just when they start to think that maybe they should fit in a bit more, they should realize *that those who fit in get lost in the crowd and never get seen.* The following are a few of my basic teachings on helping you to be YOU. I hope they give you some insight into how precious you are.

Being Seen For Who You Are

... is the only way to be seen.

It is very important for the people in your life to see you for *who you are,*
not who they think you should be.
They do not need to agree with everything you do and say,
but they must appreciate the core of who you are.

In a relationship, if you are not seen for who you are,
you will never be whole.
If you are contented with being seen as
someone else's version of who you are,
you will always feel empty and less than who you are.

If who you are doesn't work for someone, you let them walk away.
End of story. No pretending, no charade, no negotiation.
In order to be seen for who you are, you first need to see yourself.
You need to know your beauty, your gifts, your value and your worth.
Once you can see yourself, you can allow others to see you.
If you are still hiding behind other's perceptions of you,
you have a long way to go.

When you are ready to be seen for the beautiful person you are,
you show your true colors to the world.
And *when you can show your true colors to the world,*
you attract those people who will most admire those colors in you.

Are you ready to be seen or
are you still hiding behind others' perceptions of you?
Others' perceptions come and go; you are the one left standing.
Whose perception is it going to be?

It Doesn't Matter Who Believes In You

... as long as you believe in you.

When it comes to living your life, YOU are the authority.
Never give the power over to anyone else to make you feel badly about yourself.

No one has control over your life unless you give it to them.
If you give your power over to other people to prioritize their judgments
or opinions of you, then you lose yourself.
You have no one but yourself to blame if you choose to buy into others'
opinions over your own. It is always a choice.

No one's judgments or opinions should matter to you
unless they support your view of yourself.
If they do not, they should be kindly disregarded.
Don't waste your time feeling insulted, misunderstood or slighted.
It is not worth your energy. Every time you choose to put your energy there,
you take it away from building the beautiful being that you are
and/or want to become.

It's your life and your path to walk every day.
Those people will always come and go into your life,
but you will be the one left standing and upholding their judgments/
opinions long after they've left.

So ask yourself if that is what you want to be doing.
Make a better life for yourself and decide today that
you will only accept perceptions that are authentic to you and
which support your positive growth.
If those perceptions do not support your growth,
throw them out and replace them with more suitable options.

The only things we have in lives are our choices. Learn to choose wisely and
not give your power over to anyone else to malign you or take you down.
Life is too short to play out other people's perceptions of you.
Time to live your own.

To Be a Beautiful Snowflake

... you have to stand out in the cold.

And no one likes to stand out in the cold.
It usually means that you are alone and uncomfortable.

But the snowflake can only exist out in the cold.
It is the only place that can support it.

We are all beautiful snowflakes — one-of-a-kind, original and unique. We can only thrive and be ourselves when we stand out in the cold and stand up for who we are.
It is not always convenient and not always comfortable but
always necessary in the evolution of our lives.

Being who you are means respecting your needs, wants, interests and fears —
the whole package - and standing up for it
even if it is inconvenient and uncomfortable.
There will even be times when you will be
unpopular or even misunderstood.

No one should ever doubt themselves, their worth or their value.
Everyone is unique and beautiful in their own right and
everyone is worth fighting for. To truly be that beautiful snowflake,
you have to stand out in the cold.
It's easy to stay inside in the warmth.
It's harder to take a stand and defend who you are by taking the road less traveled.

After all, the cold isn't for everyone;
the cold will certainly filter out just the right people for you.
Do you want to be like everyone else and take the easy way out or
do you want to stand out in the cold and take a stand to be yourself?
The rest of your life awaits your decision. Who will you be?

Lemmings Follow

... they never lead.

We spend a good portion of our lives giving away our power to others.
We don't always make up our own minds;
we allow them to be swayed by other's viewpoints.
Sometimes it's much easier to adopt a given school of thought
than it is to apply your own intelligence to a situation.
*But every time you do that, you disempower yourself and
lose a part of your identity.*

Your work in this life is to *live YOUR life. No one else's.*
If you are waiting to see what everyone else is doing or saying
then you are not leading your life. You are leading someone else's.

You are an individual and you were NEVER meant to recede into the
background as just part of the crowd; *you were ALWAYS meant to stand out.*
Why are you hiding behind others' approvals or judgments?

The beauty is in being YOU. Not in being part of a group.
Step aside from the group and shine your light.
Your uniqueness is what makes you who you are.
Why would you ever hide from that?

*When you live your own life and make your own choices and decide NOT
to follow the crowd, your life soars in amazing ways.*
The universe is waiting to see whether you are ready to take responsibility
for your life and truly own it or if you prefer to sit it out in the passenger seat.
The rewards only come by being YOU, not by sitting it out and
watching the world go by.

Leaders make a difference in the world.
Followers are just along for the ride. Which one do you want to be?

Speak Up

... or no one will ever hear you.

Our words are extremely powerful, yet we do not know how to use them.
Generally speaking, we stuff them down and don't say
what we really want to say for fear of what others will think of us.

*Your work is to be able to be honest with yourself and then
honestly communicate yourself to others.*
You don't win any points in life by holding back and not speaking your mind.
When you hold back, you become a pawn in someone else's play.
And you are not here to live out someone else's drama.

You are here to live YOUR PLAY, no one else's. No one loses but you
when you choose to NOT express yourself adequately.
Now, that does not mean to unleash fury onto people, but it does expect
that *you speak your mind kindly, constructively and compassionately.*
When you can do that, you have done all you can to ensure a
positive outcome in your own play.

The words we use can either make or break us.
But the words we DON'T USE never have the chance to help us.

Aren't you tired of censoring yourself? Your feelings are important and
your expression of your emotions leads to your evolution, so start talking.
Your world cannot change around you if you are not communicating with others.
After all, people are not mind readers and it is not their job
to try and guess how you are feeling.
*It is your job to express yourself kindly, constructively and compassionately
(without censorship) – then your work is done.*

You only get one life (this time around); don't waste it holding your tongue.
Things don't get better by holding your tongue;
they get better through clear, kind and constructive communication.

Allowing Your Buttons To Be Pushed

... makes you part of someone else's story.

We all have our own story to manage but when we allow our "buttons" to be pushed by others, we ditch our own story in favor of starring in someone else's.
And why would we want to co-star in someone else's drama?

We all have button-pushers in our lives (usually family and significant others). The ability to identify these culprits and their button-pushing strategies is the key to owning your power and putting it back into YOU.
You should never allow yourself to feel undermined, compromised or disrespected by others.
If you notice this behavior and you notice that your reaction is to fight back, then STOP, take a breath, step back from the situation and take yourself out of that story. Clearly, it is not your story.
By fighting venom with venom, you pull yourself down into that person's story and it is a long way back to yourself.

The degree to which you will live a balanced and harmonious life is the degree to which you allow yourself to stay focused on YOUR story.
Pull back your power and put it where it belongs – into YOU.
Your happiness and equanimity of mind is found in the way you react to others.
Allowing your buttons to be pushed is a way to guarantee that you will never be emotionally balanced and free.

It's your story, no one else's. You can only control your story, no one else's.
So stop co-starring in other peoples' stories and take the lead role in your own.
Your story will end in a much better production with a much happier ending.

Comparisons Don't Feed The Soul

... yet we do it anyway.

In life it only matters who YOU are and what YOU are doing with your life.
It doesn't matter what anyone else is doing.

When we get caught up in comparing ourselves to others,
we dilute the dynamic energy of the self and divert it into negative states
such as jealousy, envy and resentment.
Those states of behavior are very deconstructive and counterproductive.
They keep you small, stuck and spiraling in the wrong direction.
*Envying someone for what they have keeps you locked in a state of "wanting and
lack,"* which is fear-based. When you focus on the Self and your dreams,
aspirations and hopes (love based),
you open yourself up to the many opportunities around you.

*Things flow easily to you when you focus on the Self whereas
when you are focused on what others have, you are locked in a state of lack.*
Because of that, you keep the very things that you seek far from you.

Time spent looking outside of ourselves for our own worth is wasted.
Comparisons do not feed the soul.
They do not feed the energy of where it is you want to be in your life.
They do the exact opposite – they throw you backwards and lock you
into a "wanting" pattern that is hard to get out of.

Believe that you already have everything that you want and need.
Visualize yourself as having the life you want and
borrow a tiny bit from that vision every day to make it a reality.

We do not get what we want in life by wishing someone else did not have it.
We only get it by believing that we ourselves have the ability to create it
for ourselves. Use the people around you as inspiration for you to have the same.
Do not begrudge them; bless them and say to yourself,
"I admire their lifestyle. I will have that as well," and then watch the doors
begin to open. Learn to reframe the situation –
turn your resentment into inspiration. It is the key to having the life you want.

What You Buy Into Is Yours

... make sure you want it.

The way in which we see things in life determines what is REAL for us – *perception is reality.* It can be no other way. Just like you can buy into a concept or buy a material object, you can buy into a thought form just as easily. If you allow yourself to identify with the mind and buy into its thought projections, you OWN them and allow them to become your own.

If you do not like the thoughts that you are experiencing,
do not give them any credence by energizing them. Let them go.
A thought is just a thought; it is not who you are unless
you have given over your control to it.

If you begin to buy into the thoughts that others hold about you, you will begin to own them and you will start identifying with them for better or worse. For example, if you are worried that your boss doesn't think very highly of the work you are doing, you will begin to identify with that thought form and begin to manifest it.

What you buy into is yours. Before making any purchase, it is first wise to do the work... do you identify with this thought?
Is it constructive to be identifying with this thought?
Will this thought form be beneficial to your life if you choose to buy into it?
It is wise to remember that any and all thoughts are just that... thoughts.
They have absolutely no bearing on your life unless you allow it.
Why turn over the keys when you are the one who is best qualified to be driving?
Get back into the drivers seat, take back control of your mind and only buy into the thoughts that YOU want to own.

Growing Roots In Salty Soil

... never works.

Everyone knows that plants do not grow in salty soil,
yet in our own lives we often times find ourselves
trying to establish roots in a foundation or a community
that is not the most supportive of our needs.

In life, it is important to know who we are and what we want and need
out of life. Once we know that,
we can find the optimal soil conditions to help ourselves flourish.
Problems arise when we do not ask ourselves who we are and
what we need to grow and become the best we can be.
We mistakenly pot ourselves into many beds,
many of which never support our dreams, hopes or aspirations.
Sometimes those pots are even poisonous to us,
yet we are continually attracted to their brightly colored patterns.
Each time we think, "Oh, it is such a pretty pot, it has to be right for me!
How could it not be?" *Sometimes we try and make things*
other than the way they are.
We try and fool ourselves by telling ourselves that the person we are in
relationship with is actually the right one for us or
that our job is actually fulfilling us on every level necessary.
It is much easier to make excuses for bad soil then it is to pull ourselves out of the
toxic bed and replant in healthy supportive soil.

Why expect the impossible? Why not be realistic as to the environment
that you require to truly thrive?
Once you can recognize that the salty soil is holding you back from
becoming the best you can be and, in many cases, may be killing you completely,
then you can make a better choice for yourself.
The only pots you want to plant yourself in are the ones where you see
great opportunity for growth and happiness.
If the soil looks or feels dead to you, get out of the pot.
There are many pots just waiting to be explored -
no sense in sitting in dead soil. Happy potting!

Giving Away Your Power

... renders you powerless.

Yet we all do it.

When you give your power over to another human being to judge you,
you weaken yourself.
We spend too much time caring too much what other people think about us.
"Do they think I am intelligent? Do they think I am good at my job?
Do they think I am a good match for him/her?
Do they respect the work I do? And so forth.

It doesn't matter what other people think about you;
it only matters what YOU think.

Every time you worry about others' opinions about you,
you give your energy over to them to fret over their opinions.
That exchange of energy only leaves you depleted, depressed and defeated.
Time to pull it back. Take back your power and override your fears of
others' judgments. When you take back your energy,
you empower yourself to put that energy back into yourself and
your work. The results will speak for themselves.

When we give our power over to others, we become powerless ourselves.
No more giving your power over to others to feel badly about yourself.
Time to stop undermining who you are and start owning your own power.
Focus not on how others view you, but on what YOU have to contribute to the world.
Your opinions are the only ones that matter.
When you put your energy back into YOU, your world shines and
everyone sees you as the star you always were.

Self-Love,
Self-Worth & Self-Esteem

Once you know who you are,
the goal is to *learn to love, honor and respect yourself.*

If you lack self-love, self-worth and self-esteem,
you lack the tools necessary to play your best hand in life.

After all, if you do not love yourself, how can you love
another person and more importantly,
how can you allow yourself to be loved by another?

When you truly learn to love and value yourself and
value your importance in relationships, the dynamic changes and
the doors to love, abundance and happiness open up in amazing ways.
In life, loving and valuing yourself is a game changer.
So go ahead and give yourself the winning advantage.
Don't you think you deserve it?

Chapter 2

Self-Love, Self-Worth & Self-Esteem

This trilogy is definitely one of the most complicated life lesson packages one can take on in a lifetime. There is no easy way around it; most people do not love themselves nor do they believe in themselves nor honor themselves. It's sad, but if you ask many people, they will tell you that of course they love themselves and value themselves, but in reality, they will overcompensate with ego. The tendency is to over-inflate the ego to seem bigger and better than one's own abilities. That is a scapegoat for not doing the work on yourself. Never confuse self-love with ego.

Real self-love, self-worth and self-esteem is humble. It has nothing to prove. It does not come from an ego place of fear, but a place of love and of service. It is vulnerable.

Real self-love, self-worth and self-esteem is about loving oneself – supremely, honestly and humbly. Once again, it is not about the ego. It is not about being selfish or self centered. It is about giving to oneself first, so that one has even more to give to others.

Real self-love, self-worth and self-esteem honors itself and protects itself by asserting boundaries. These boundaries are established upfront so respect is required and upheld and one never allows oneself to be walked on.

It must be said that this package is definitely one of my most difficult life lessons. As a natural nurturer, my tendency is to give, give and give more. I have since learned that giving everything is not a sign of nurturing, but a sign of *lack of self-love* and *self-worth*. True self-love, self-worth and self-esteem loves itself unconditionally, but loves itself primarily. Once again, it's not about being selfish or self-centered, but is all about the loving of oneself, so that one has more to give to others. It is a delicate balance and one that I have consciously been working on over the last 20+ years of my life.

Learning to love myself has been a journey into understanding myself and who I am, how special I am and what it is I need for myself and from others in a relationship. Truly loving myself has been a quest into asking myself what it is I need to be happy and how I can give that to myself, since I am supremely the one in charge of my own happiness. But, at the same token, it is also a process of learning to ask for my needs to be met while in a relationship with someone. My tendency is to address my own needs and not ask for my needs to be met because I do not want to put pressure on the other person. But true self-love, self-worth and self-esteem honors itself and puts its need first in a relationship. It is only by honoring oneself, that one can truly be able to honor the relationship. I always tell clients that *if you accept crumbs*

Chapter 2

Self-Love, Self-Worth & Self-Esteem

from someone, those crumbs will never give you a whole loaf of bread and they certainly will never give you the full bakery that you deserve. And what's worse is that those crumbs are just enough to keep you starving and desperate for more. It's almost better to give up those crumbs and let your stomach shrink until you attract the full loaf of bread that you deserve.

The following essays are my foundational teachings on what it means to really love yourself and secure true self-worth and self-esteem along the way. These inspirational words have helped me along my journey and I hope they will inspire you along your journey into loving yourself and valuing your needs.

When You Love Yourself

... you win.

When you give to YOU, you have so much more to give to others –
your light shines.

When you continually put others and their needs in front of yours,
you suffer – it puts out your light.

Believe it or not, your only responsibility in life is to yourself. That is not to say that
you become selfish. But it is to say that your goal in life should be
to prioritize your needs and *NOT push them to the back burner for anyone.*

Our goal in life is to become healthy, happy and well-adjusted.
This only happens by honoring ourselves and our boundaries with others.
*When you are good to YOU, your vibration raises, you feel fulfilled, contented, supported
and inspired to live the best life you can.* It is from that space that we can create
happiness and success while also inspiring others
to make positive changes in their lives.

But when we overextend ourselves and give everything away to others
(aka becoming the "martyr"), we take ourselves down.
When you give yourself away, you lose YOU.
A simple concept that we have yet to embrace.
No one told you that you are responsible for saving the world.
You want to do good in the world? Start by saving yourself FIRST.
Draw real boundaries between you and negative people who drag you
down, take time out for yourself, treat yourself to anything that makes you happy.
Honor YOU, and watch your life flourish. Like attracts like.
When you are happy, your vibration raises and you continue to attract
high vibrational people and situations into your life.

*But when you are busy exploiting yourself for others, your vibration drops and you
continue to attract lower vibrational situations and people.*
How do you want to live? Learn to love yourself and make the most out of
YOUR life. *No one is responsible for your happiness but you, so make it a priority.*

Believing In Yourself

... is a game changer.

And who doesn't want to change the rules of the game in their favor?

Believing in yourself is the ultimate secret to success in life.
The problem is that many of us do not believe in ourselves. In life,
*those who are the most intelligent and most gifted are usually the ones who doubt
themselves the most.* They know too much and therefore realize that there is
so much more that they still do not know.
Because of that, they are the first to undermine themselves and
feel inadequate and unable to compete.

On the other hand, ignorance is always bliss. *Those who do not know as much
are usually the ones that blindly charge into opportunities because they have no fear of
not knowing enough.* They do not know any better so they always go for it —
the "fool" in the tarot, to be exact. They believe in themselves
simply because they do not overthink situations.
Since they do not know that they do not know,
they take more chances and put it out there more easily.

When you STOP judging yourself and stop applying negative energy such
as doubt and fear to situations, you will succeed.
Don't question your intention or your ability to do something; just do it.
You are the only one standing in your way. If you are going to apply
thought to situations, *why not apply positive thinking to support where you want to
go in life?* As soon as negative thinking steps in, you hold yourself back.

Welcome to the game of life — believing in yourself is the game changer.
Get with the program and learn the strategy.
Choose NOT to believe in your limitations but *believe in your dreams* and
they will always come true.

Are You Open?

... you might not be.

Just because you want something, doesn't mean you get it.
You have to be OPEN to receiving it.
You have to feel WORTHY of having it and
you have to be a VIBRATIONAL MATCH to it
before it can appear in your life.
Getting what you want is a process.
And until you gel with that process, what you want will always elude you.

Many of us do not have what we want in our lives because on some level we do not feel worthy of having it. Maybe we feel inadequate for that job promotion.
Maybe we feel that the object of our affections is "out of our league."
Maybe we feel we do not have enough or the right education to do what we really want to do in life. Maybe, maybe, maybe...
but just maybe it's all of our maybes that are keeping us back from having everything we truly want.
Maybe doesn't guarantee success. By nature, it is littered with doubt.
Telling yourself you might not get it assures you never will.
Being truly open means acknowledging that it is there for you and anxiously awaiting its arrival with a certainty that it is yours.

So remember, isolating what you want is the easy part. Now the real work begins.
Before what you want can make it into your reality, you must be able to embody the energy of being truly open to it. In other words, knowing you are worthy of having it and allowing yourself to live in a space where excitement is bringing it to your door.
Is there something you want? Learn to be open to receiving it...

Know you are worth it.

Get excited about having it.

Never ponder the possibility of it not happening.

That way, your work is done, and it will most certainly be yours. Are you ready to receive what you truly want? Time to be open to it.

Being a Doormat

... gets you walked on.

There's no way around it. If you roll out a doormat outside your front door, people will naturally step all over it. And why not? That's what it's there for.

The same holds with your personal relationships – all relationships. *It all comes down to personal boundaries.* How clear are you with your boundaries? Do you let others cross them from time to time? Do you tend to take the path of least resistance and give others the benefit of the doubt? Do you like to refrain from "rocking the boat?" That is all wonderful *until conceding becomes compromising.*

Being nice doesn't win you the race. Being authentic to yourself does. It's very simple. If you allow others to walk all over you – even just once – you are telling the universe that you do not deserve better and that you are OK with a given state of behavior.

You should NEVER be OK with taking a back seat to bad behavior. Being nice does NOT negate the energy of accepting less than you deserve. *The only thing that will change bad behavior is enforcing boundaries.* If you set up your boundaries upfront, people will know that there are boundaries in existence and that they cannot be crossed. But if you never establish boundaries, others will push the edges to see how far they can go. It is human nature.

If you do not want to be walked on, take the doormat off the front porch. Explain to your guests as they come in that in your house, guests take off their shoes. After all, it's YOUR house and they should abide by YOUR rules. Establish those rules upfront and you will find that in life, people will seldom cross them, or will at least think twice about crossing them.

... makes sure it never gets crossed.

Relationships are about boundaries. When relating to others, it is critical
that you are extremely clear about your boundaries and
what behavior you will accept and what behavior you will NOT accept.

Often times we get upset with others' behavior.
We feel slighted by their words or their actions. Unfortunately, it is too easy
to turn a blind eye and hope the other person is having an off day.
Either that, or we react the opposite way and unconsciously explode into a
fit of victimizing anger. Neither action yields the desired result.

Communication upfront is the only way to ensure that your needs will be met.
Don't expect others to know what "good and fair" behavior is for you.
Don't give them the opportunity to decide that.
It is your work to decide what you will and will not accept from others.

Once you are clear with your boundaries, you will be met with much BETTER outcomes.
When people are clear with their boundaries, other people respect them more.
They respect them for respecting themselves. *In other words, you get much
better behavior when you establish the expectation upfront.*

There will always be people who push your boundaries and try to cross
the line. If you haven't set up the line beforehand, it will always make it
harder to distinguish later. Also, if you haven't designated the line at all,
how can others know when they have crossed it?
Be clear with your boundaries. Learn to speak up for yourself.
Learn to defend your integrity and let no one cross that line.

You get what you accept. If you do not want to accept it, do not allow it.
You cannot control others' behavior, but you can control what you will
and will not accept from them. Avoidance does not solve the issue,
nor does arguing. Communicating yourself upfront – kindly, constructively and compassionately - will go so far in supporting
the type of interactions you will receive in your life.
Love yourself. Respect yourself and draw the line.

If the line is there, others will most certainly think twice about crossing it.

Fake It 'Til You Make It

... it's the only way to become real.

Nobody ever thinks they are ready to embark on something new.
In your mind, you will never have enough money to have your first child,
or move into that big new home, or buy your beach house, or get married
or change your career. You will always tell yourself that something is first
needed before you can make that move.
This is your ego's way of keeping you safe from a perceived failure.
For most of us, *we would prefer to never try than to try and fail.*
The ego is clever; it comes fully equipped with defense mechanisms to
protect it from looking foolish or "less than perfect."
This shows up as procrastination measures, and procrastination ultimately
marks the difference between surviving and thriving.

Adhering to the ego keeps you small and keeps you from becoming great.
Most great opportunities in life force us to grow and move beyond our comfort zones.
Feeling comfortable is a sign to you that you have conquered and
achieved. *Feeling discomfort is a sign to you that you need to persevere and challenge yourself.*
The choice is always yours. Life never happens to you – *it happens for you.*
The secret is in believing in yourself.
Even if you think you do not have what it takes, you keep moving forward.
Fake it 'til you make it – then it will be yours.
By taking on the challenge with an air of certainty and belief in yourself,
you will always earn that which you are seeking.

If You Are Not Where You Want To Be

... pick it up.

No one is responsible for your happiness but YOU.
You are the only one holding yourself back.
Your obstacles to greatness are all imagined.
Don't allow your fears to keep you from being the best you can be.

There are no victims in life.
There are only those who do not want to rise to their life lessons.

If you find your life is not where you want it to be,
do whatever you need to do to get it there.
The actions you take will always reap benefits.
It is the inaction that creates resistance to what you want.
In other words, the energy of action (any action) moves you forward,
and the energy of inaction creates stagnancy.

You can have whatever you want in life.
You just have to pick it up and make it happen.
The more you allow yourself to sit out on the bench and
watch others succeed while feeling badly about yourself,
the more you stay stuck.

Giving up never gets you what you want.
Getting out there in any capacity will always change the dynamic for you.
Don't think you need the perfect strategy to succeed. You only need to
get up off the ground and make a move – any move. That move supports
your intention to succeed, and the universe will respond in kind.

Life is too short to wait for your dreams to come true.
If your life isn't exactly where you want it to be right now, do something about it.
The action of intention will always bring you success.
The stronger your actions, the stronger the level of change you will bring about.
What are you waiting for? Your best life is waiting for you –
get out there and make a move.

People With Big Egos

... take up MORE space.

They just do. It doesn't mean that they are better than anyone else; it's just that they take up MORE space.

People with smaller egos need to occupy the same space as the bigger egos. Herein is the issue. *Smaller ego types tend to get pushed out of the room as they have not yet learned how to hold their ground with the big ego.*

Either way, smaller egos are generally two types – either extremely accomplished *yet humble evolved beings,* OR they are individuals who do not yet believe in themselves and allow the big egos to push them out of the room.

Small egos can become resentful, angry and bitter towards the big egos who generally do not even realize the smaller egos are in the same room with them. The small egos feel as if they are being overlooked, marginalized and pushed out of the room.
This is only so because the small ego is ALLOWING IT.

In life, both egos have to co-exist in the same room. Big egos take up more space so it is up to the small ego to learn to hold its ground. The small ego does not have to compete with the big ego, *it just has allow itself to be who it is and believe in itself and STAND UP FOR ITSELF and carve out that space that it needs to do its life's work.*

Nothing comes out of allowing a big ego to push you out the door. As a small ego, you lose, and the big ego has more room to puff itself up and feel good about itself. There is no competition here.
It doesn't matter how "small" you are; it matters how well you can hold your space in the presence of a big ego. You do not have to be a big ego to hold space with a big ego, you just have to hold the space YOU NEED and never allow it to be compromised. Don't spend your time resenting a big ego, recognize that there is great strength and beauty in *small packages.*
As long as the package is strong in itself, it will always give the big package a run for its money.

You Are Not Broken

... just a bit bent.

Life's challenges may throw you to the ground and stomp all over you,
but *you will never be broken.* You will, of course, wear your war wounds,
but they are *your badge of courage, wisdom and life experience.*
They make you who you are. You are never damaged goods
if you see life's trials and tribulations as a means to improve upon yourself
and make your life better.

You are not broken; you are only bent. In life, you WANT to be bent.
No one lives the straight and narrow path. That's boring.
Without life's twists and turns and falls from grace, you wouldn't be who you are today.
You do not want to be the straight arrow – that represents a life not lived.
The nature of life is to "rough you up" and "take you down."
This cycle never breaks you because after awhile
you learn how to fall and your scars heal quicker.

You are not broken, but your path has to be.
Learning how to jump the cracks and navigate the holes of life makes you stronger.
Life may beat you down from time to time,
but you can always rest in the understanding that
being bent means you have lived, loved, learned and experienced a richness
that will make your life that much better.

No one wants to live the straight and narrow.
Respect yourself for all your life-earned war wounds.
In being bent, you are acknowledging your unique life path and
those lessons that have gotten you to where you are today.
Being bent is a gift and a reflection of a life well-lived.
It means you have the innate ability to stand up to life's hardships
while demonstrating the ability to translate your troubled path into
a life of real meaning and rich reward.
Now, that's worth a little bending!

Life is a Game

Once you know who you are,
and you have learned to fully love and value yourself,
the goal is to *learn the rules of the game.*

The big secret about life is that it is a game.

It doesn't matter whether you win or lose,
it only matters how you play it.

Learn to arm yourself with the tools you need to help you
play your best hand, whatever that is for you.

Chapter 3

Life is a Game

I used to always be at the mercy of whatever was going on in my life at any given moment. If the situation was good, I could be happy, and if it was bad, I was undoubtedly unhappy. I allowed the situations in my life to dictate my happiness. This was one of my big mistakes. I have since learned that *happiness is a choice*. And it is a choice that we can make every day.

When I started to wake up and understand the ways in which the universe worked through me, I realized that all situations (especially the painful ones) were only happening to me in order to bring me to a better place. My work was to make sure I could reframe those situations in my life to help me to get the lesson from it and get out so I could move forward in my life. So instead of allowing myself to be the victim of the situation and let the lesson beat me up, I learned to ask myself what the lesson was here. That process allowed me to become the master of my life and helped me to evolve and learn to play a better game in the game of life.

A very personal example would be that of my breakup with my soon-to-be life partner whom I mentioned earlier. He was, and is to this day, a beautiful man; perfect in so many ways, but when push came to shove, in terms of being a committed partner, he was a cheat. OK, no judgments; when we look at the facts, he made a very impulsive decision to jump out of our relationship, which, I will add, was NOT broken. I mean, we had issues like any other couple but we had such a strong connection and solid communication foundation that we could have worked through anything and always did.

Now, it might help if I explain to you that he was working through some tough life lessons including: *fear of commitment, fear of intimacy* and *fear of being controlled.* He was 42 at the time and had never been married or engaged (definitely a sign!). I knew about his fears. He always clearly communicated them to me (as we always shared our feelings quite openly about everything).

Now, obviously I am not perfect either, I came to the table with my own life lessons which tend to be around *self-esteem, self-worth* and *self-love.* I tend to sacrifice self for others and I used to think that doing so was an expression of "being of service" to others and a means of being nurturing and unselfish. No, it was just a statement of lack of self-worth.

So really, the dissolution of our relationship was a perfect storm of all of our life lessons colliding. Had we both been working on our personal lessons we would have

Chapter 3

Life is a Game

had a much different result. How, you might ask?

Well, it's important to remember that in life, *nothing is as it appears to be*. It would seem that my ex's actions to leave me for another woman would make him the "villain" here as most of our friends and family had attested to. But that wouldn't be an accurate assessment. Yes, he was very callous and very impetuous (not to mention cruel) by only spending time with her for two weeks before deciding that he wanted to be with her. He was willing to risk everything, end our two-year relationship and throw me out of our apartment for this new situation. There was never a discussion of problems we may have had/needed to work through, no discussion of either of us ever being unhappy in the relationship or ever having our needs not met. It was really a simple situation of a myna bird seeing something shiny in its path and wanting it.

Remember, he is programmed towards a *fear of commitment, fear of intimacy* and *a fear of being controlled*. It would help to tell you that a couple months prior, I had lost my full time job and he was paying our rent because I didn't make/have any money. I was very grateful and as a result of feeling completely disempowered, I fell into my patterns of *lack of self-worth, self-esteem*, and I started to over-nurture him while not taking care of myself. I put his needs first and did everything for him (maybe even mothered him). I thought he was more worthy of my attention and affections than I was. I would clean the apartment and cook every meal for him. I was trying to show my gratitude but really this isn't who I am (a housewife I am NOT!) but when my fears come up, I fall into this sabotaging pattern of putting other's needs ahead my own. In my subconscious pattern, it was much easier to take care of him then it was for me to look in the mirror and ask myself the very difficult question of what I was going to do with the rest of my life. It was a form of escapism to focus on him and avoid having to tackle the issues of my low self-esteem and self-worth.

Regardless, he didn't want to be the focus of my attention; it made him uncomfortable, it suffocated him and brought up his need to flee from commitment. And he had since lost his full-time job as well, so we were living and working together in our apartment, in our own hotbed of lessons! There you have it. The universe brought up a testing period for both of us. Had I been working on my issues of *self-esteem, self-worth* and *self-love*, I would not have exhibited suffocating behavior and started to press on his issues of *fear of commitment, fear of intimacy and fear of being controlled*. I would have been too busy job searching and planning my next move to empower myself. At the same token, had he been working on his issues, he would have been better able to recognize that I wasn't trying to control and mother him, but was in need of putting my attention back into myself and empowering myself. He wouldn't have felt triggered or intimidated by my nurturing actions towards him. He would have been able to step outside his fears and not allow them to overcome him.

Woulda, shoulda, coulda… doesn't matter; we took the bait that was handed to us (this new woman thrown into our equation) and we failed all our lessons miserably, but we failed them TOGETHER. Despite what everyone (including myself) wanted to see back then, he was not the bad guy here; that was the easy answer and very much NOT the correct one. He was not "wrong" in cheating, throwing me out and being harshly cruel in the way he did it. That was my painful consequence for not rising to my lessons. In fact, it was all happening to bring BOTH of us to a better place.

Today, he has learned the consequences of his actions as he realized only a few short months later that he had made the biggest mistake of his life (letting me go) and had since tried to get me back over a three-year period. I forgave him wholeheartedly, but unfortunately was unable to ever forget it, even though I really wanted to. He learned his lessons and will never do this to another woman. As for me, I learned that not taking care of myself and putting other's needs over my own is always a losing strategy. It taught me that when you love yourself, YOU WIN. I will never again prioritize anyone's needs over my own. I love myself too much to sacrifice my needs. I am special and important and someone to be valued. More importantly, I learned what it is to truly believe in my worth because I had to recreate myself from the ground up after the destruction and boy, was it hard earned! So, lessons learned, and we are BOTH better for having had this experience.

Now, I will say this: catching your lessons is NOT easy. It requires focus and consciousness in every moment. We are not conditioned that way. In our fast-paced society, we barely remember what we had for dinner last night, let alone be mindful enough to catch a repetitive lesson showing up in our lives. It is much easier for us to fall into those repetitive patterns of behavior and sleepwalk our way through our lives, but that never solves anything – it just sets us up for a harsh wake-up call. And I will be honest with you, those calls really s--- when they come calling!

But once you learn that *nothing is as it appears to be and that everything that is happening in your life is only happening for you to learn something, then you begin to empower yourself and*

Chapter 3

Life is a Game

take charge of your lessons rather than allowing your lessons to run over you. It is a much more constructive approach to your life and one which will ensure your emotional development while subsequently sending you the rewards you deserve.

Ready to start? The following essays are my foundational teachings for helping you to learn to play the game of life. These simple rules will help you to understand how to play the game and how you can make better moves to get what you want/need out of your own life.

Life is a Game

... you only need to know how to play it.

It doesn't matter if you win or lose, what matters is how you play the game.

If we could see that our lives are perfectly orchestrated by us,
we would not put so much stock in external drama.
We buy into our illusions as being real — all the day-to-day drama seems
overwhelming at times and we think we might not make it through.

The fact is, we are always in control.
We are the ones orchestrating all the moves on the table.
Sure, we may make a bad move here or there, and we may even lose a
game or two, but *the winning is in the learning behind every bad move.*
We learn the most from our bad moves and our opponent's bad moves.
Never despair; *there is always another game to be played and
always another opportunity to make a different move.*

In the game of life, the king or the queen can always be taken out.
But we are never the king or the queen that gets taken out,
we have to remember that we are bigger than that.
We are the ones with free will and we are the ones
who are making the moves that affect our lives everyday.
We are in control. As long as we are in this body,
we are in complete control of every move we make.
We are never the pieces getting dragged off the board.

Remember that you are never a victim of your life. You are the one strategizing
your next move at every given moment.
Ultimately, it's not about winning or losing.
The wins are always in the lessons, never in the number of pieces left on the board.

When The Dust Settles

... you can see more clearly.

But not until then.

We all go through really confusing situations from time to time.
And while you are going through them, they never make sense.
They are NOT supposed to. At the time, you just need to get through them.
But once the dust settles, you can begin to understand just why
that situation was happening to you.

Clarity only comes with time. Take a step back from those painful, confusing
situations and put your energy into something else.
All the wanting in the world for answers will NOT *bring them any quicker.*
Situations resolve and lessons are learned when the timing is right.

Let the chaos around you settle down; don't try and force the dust to settle either.
You cannot control the amount of time you are caught in that dust storm.
So best to put on your goggles and gear and trudge onwards.
The important thing is that you nurture yourself along the way.
All dust storms create uncertainty, confusion and, of course, bring up fear of the unknown.
But as long as you know that going in to the drama, then you can remind
yourself that the dust isn't forever; it is just an illusion.
Before you know it, that the dust will settle and
you will have complete clarity.

Life is a process and everyone gets caught in the dust storm;
the question is, how do you ride it out? Don't take it too seriously;
the dust will settle and you will see what was there for you all along.
You don't always get what you want in life, but you always get what you need.
Once the dust settles, you can see what that is.

Stop Chasing The Wrong Things

... and give the right things a chance to catch up with you.

In life, it is very common to chase the "wrong" things.
We have a tendency to chase the things we actually do not want in our lives.
Why would anyone do that, you may ask?
Well, it is rarely ever done consciously, that is for sure.
You see, everything in life is energy.
Wherever you are putting your thoughts or intentions,
that is where your energy goes.
Where your energy goes is what you end up "chasing."
It seems to be a complex equation, but a very simple outcome.
If you do not want someone or something in your life, do NOT give it any attention.
It is as easy as that. Do not expend your precious energy on manifesting
that which does not make you happy.

When you continually mull over a person or situation that has wronged
you in the past, you keep your energy locked to that person or situation
(for better or worse).
When your energy is locked, it is not available to free flow outwards and
attract the people and the situations you really do want in your life.
It is otherwise occupied. In essence, *you end up subconsciously "chasing" after
the things you do not want.* If you know they are not what you want,
it is time to cut your ties to the past which will only ever hold you back
and shift your energy forwards.
Think ahead, think new, dream big... this will help bring you new situations
and encounters that will more realistically match your needs.

Everything is energy. *Looking at the past keeps you locked in it.*
Break the binds that tie you to the past and stop chasing what you do not
want in life. *Allow yourself to attract that which you do want and give it a chance
to successfully catch up to you.* In life we are meant to have everything we
have ever wanted, but we subconsciously keep ourselves and our energy
pre-occupied with what we do not want/need in our lives.
Life is too short to lament past mistakes and misfortunes.
The future, with all your dreams, is available at every moment.
Seize the day and allow real happiness to catch up with you.

If You Want a Better Garden

... plant better seeds.

Nothing will grow in your garden unless it's *nurtured and nourished.*

Often times we complain about not having what it is we want in life, but we don't realize that it's by our own hand.

It is very simple...

If something is important in your life, you have to nurture it.

If you do not nurture it, you will lose it.

If you lose it, you have no one to blame but yourself.

Beautiful gardens do not just grow on their own.
They require *the right seeds, quality time, patience, and most importantly, a dedication to nurturing.*

Ask yourself what is it that you are lacking in your life?
And what seeds are you planting to correct that?
If all you are doing is complaining about what you don't have,
I assure you, you will never have it. *You never just get what you want because you think you deserve it.* You will only get it if you put the necessary seeds and subsequent nurturing into place allowing it to grow and prosper in your life.

Lifeless gardens never yield bountiful harvests.
If there is something you want in your life, plant the right seeds and learn to nurture them into being. When you do the work, your life's garden will blossom beyond your wildest imagination.

Life Is a Process

... to bring you to where you need to be.

There isn't anywhere else to go.

There is NO perfect place. There is NOWHERE you need to be.
You have only to enjoy the process of your life, step by step.

There is a divine process to your life. It has already been mapped out for you.
Your only task is to walk it. Of course, you have free will and can change
any or all of it at any moment,
but the blueprint is always in place to help navigate you.

So how does that translate to your daily life?
Believe it or not, *destiny has a funny way of finding you.*
There is a logic to your path, even though it may be hard to see.
Instead of fighting/forcing things to happen,
learn to sit back and trust in the process of your life to unfold your truth.

So, in other words…

Whatever is happening to you, is meant to be happening in that moment.

Whatever is not working in your life, is not meant to be happening in that moment.

You are NOT lost. You are NOT broken.
If you are not where you want to be, it is because it is not yet time.
Your life has a perfectly choreographed
timeline that the universe always upholds.

Even though you may not understand why you are where you are,
learn to trust the process of your life to bring you to the exact next step
you require. So, *instead of questioning where you are, learn to understand WHY
you are there.* By spotting the patterns and learning to trust your path,
your life opens in miraculous ways.
You may not have all the answers but the universe always does.
Everything always happens in its own time frame.
Learn to trust in the process of your life to
bring you where you need to be WHEN you need to be there.

There isn't anywhere else to go.

The Right Choices

... are always the hardest to make.

We all have an inner-knowing – that guide within us that secretly whispers in our ear and tells us what direction to go in life.

But do we always listen to it? It is our soul, our intuitive guide, which tells us that something is not quite right.

Even though we may know that something is not quite right, we are not always able to make the right choice for ourselves because those choices generally involve pain.

No one wants to make the choice that is going to be harder or more painful. Everyone wants to make the choice that is easier and where suffering is alleviated.

The bigger question in life is do we want to live on the "Easy Path" or on the "Path of Life."

Those who choose the "Path of Life" understand that *in the game of life, easier doesn't win you the race. The highest choices for ourselves are generally the ones that force us to grow and evolve further.* Indeed, these high choices may crash us harder and faster, BUT they transform into growth and happiness much quicker than the easier choices.

On the other hand, *the "Easy Path" is laced with easier choices and they are just that, easier.* They generally perpetuate an unsatisfactory situation for a much longer period of time. *Easier choices have a way of delaying our growth.* They keep us in a type of "bliss is ignorance" state of mind or a state of "easeful limbo," a sort of "calm before the storm." The problem is that through making easier choices, one takes the easy way out.

Now, understand that you can only hide from your lessons for so long.

It is just a matter of time before that storm hits full force and you come crashing down to the same place you would have had you made the highest choice years earlier. But this time, the pain is much more severe, and there was much more at stake.

Why do that to yourself? Why delay your progress?

Decisions made to help you avoid pain never work.

How do you know when you make the right choice?

It feels harder initially, but in the end, you reap far more benefits and you allow yourself to transform and move forward in life much more quickly.

Remember, *nothing good in life ever comes easy and nothing easy is ever really worth fighting for.*

What choice will you make next?

Getting Up Off The Bench

... puts you back in the game.

So often in life we are afraid of making a decision
for fear that it will be the wrong decision.
Sometimes we find ourselves sitting out of the game
because it is safer than to play and potentially fail.
When we opt out of the game instead of playing,
we will never know if we could have won.
We truly lose when we do not allow ourselves to play the game.
It's like the quote,
"don't let your fear of striking out keep you from playing the game."

In life it does not matter what direction you go in; it only matters that you go in a direction.
Once you are up and moving in a direction,
the universe can guide you to where you need to be.
But if you are sitting out in the sidelines and not even in the game, no one can help you.
You have to help yourself and get yourself up and moving.
Once you are moving and in the game, things start to open for you.

Don't wait for the perfect time to make a decision.
That time will never come. Every day is the perfect day to make a decision.
Every day that you choose to get up off that bench and make a choice is
one step closer to finding your true purpose and happiness.
Don't hide behind your fear of failing. The only failure you can make in
life is failing to get up off that bench and not allowing yourself
the chance to be great.

If It's Complicated

... it isn't meant to be happening right now.

It's as simple as that.

Everything happens in its own time here on planet Earth.
Just because you want something to come together now doesn't mean it will.

Your pushing for it to come together before it's time
only creates obstacles and frustration.
If it was meant to be in your life right now, it would be working out.
The fact that it isn't working out for you as quickly as you would like it to
is your indication that it is not yet ready to be in your life.

All the forceful pushing and prodding for it to manifest will not manifest
it any quicker. In fact, it will only create problems for you.
The universe is your own built-in buffer system.
*It keeps what is not ready for you at bay until
it is at a place where you can dance with it.*

If it is meant to be in your life, it comes together quite naturally with an
ease that only the universal flow can bring.
*But if it is not yet ready to be in your life, it will not come together with great ease,
there will be hardships, obstacles and delays.*
This is your indication to take a step back from the situation and
release your grip.

In actuality you do not want to force your will on yourself.
You do not want something that is not at your level.
Take back your energy and put that energy into something else.
*When it is time for that situation to manifest in your life, it will come together,
and if it doesn't, it was never going to.*

Life Does Not Hand You Everything You Want

... but it will give you what you need.

And it is usually much better.
How many of us bemoan our fate when we do not get exactly what we
were hoping for? We often like to play the underdog and say,
"Oh, woe is me, why didn't I get that new job or why did that girl/guy
leave me or why didn't 'x' work out the way I wanted it to?"

You can ask yourself these questions over and over again.
Unfortunately, it will not change the reality of the situation for you.
What we fail to realize in life is that we are never alone.
We are always guided by a divine force
that is acting on behalf of our highest good at all times.
Nothing that is right for you will ever be taken away
(unless the timing is not quite right for it to materialize).

The universe is a complex orchestration of destiny at play.
What we think is right for us seldom is. In truth, we never really know what is
right for us until years later when we look back and say,
"Oh, thank God that job was taken away from me.
I would have never left it on my own and I would have never
gone back to school and become who I am today..."

Anything that happens in your life is a blessing;
it is a God's way of moving you along your projected path.
Things may not always work out the way you would like them to,
but they work out the way they are supposed to.

You may not always get what you want in life, but you always get what
you need (whether or not you know you need it at the time).
And, in my experience, it is always better than
what you thought you wanted.
Life is funny that way.

Stop Thinking You Have All The Answers

... trust me, you don't.

If life was as easy as that, no one would ever have to come to this huge
earthly classroom of learning.
If we had all the answers to every challenge,
what would be the point of going through it?

Sometimes we get stuck on a page – the content is boring,
we can't get through the chapter, we have read the same passage over and
over again. Logic would dictate that we need to read on if change is ever
going to be found. When we learn to turn the page and push beyond the
boredom of that page, we bring new insights to the table and
we breathe a fresh outcome into our situation.

Certainty narrows and uncertainty broadens.
When you stop thinking that you have all the answers,
you free up the energy to bring you new solutions you have never even
dreamed of. Don't keep yourself trapped in your same habitual patterns.
When you learn to think outside the box, new situations, new people and
certainly new outcomes become more readily available.
When you think you know all the answers and have seen it all and done it
all, you lock yourself down in a repetitive pattern that is very dense and
heavy. When you learn to abandon your "trusted remedies," life has a way
of opening up in amazing and very surprising ways.
Let go and surrender is the name of the game –
the game that will undoubtedly yield you the greatest results.

Controlling your every move, and going through life with blinders on is
akin to sleepwalking your way through it. Why bother?
The point of life is to leverage every rich experience and to grow from
that experience. *We do not grow by repeating the same calculated strategies.*
Live your life with as much color and zest as you can muster.
Stop thinking you have all the answers, you might just learn something new.
Remember: certainty narrows, uncertainty broadens.
It is when you think you have all the answers that is just
the time to abandon ship and learn to swim!

You Don't Always Get What You Want

... you get what you choose.

And they are not always the same thing.

The only things we have in life are our choices. We live and die by them. *The quality of our life is completely contingent on the quality of the choices we make.*

How often do we complain that we are not getting our needs met in a certain relationship or at a certain job?
But how can we complain when we set it up that way?
Who is to blame, really?

In life, you will NOT always get what you want, but you will certainly get what you choose. So if your choice is not giving you the desired results you would like, it might be time to make another choice for yourself.

You are always in control of your life – at every juncture.
No one has control over your life unless you give it to them.
You are not being punished; you are not a victim of your life.
If you are not getting what you want or what you need, it is time to look at the choices you have made thus far and make some new choices.

Don't spend your time trying to change people to make them what you want or need.
That's not your job. Your job is to change yourself and the choices you make so that they better suit your needs and wants.

Life is a delicate dance of all the choices you make. So, remember, it's not about your needs and wants. *It's about what you are choosing that will determine the quality of your life.* You don't always get what you want, but you will certainly get what you choose. *So choose wisely.*

Learn to See Your Patterns

... otherwise you will repeat them.

We all have patterns, we are just not acutely aware of them.
In fact, we spend our lifetimes going through the same patterns
over and over again. It's called sleepwalking our way through our lives.
We keep hitting our head on the walls over and over again wondering,
"Why do things like this keep happening to us?"
We feel victimized by the pattern instead of empowered and
awakened to make necessary change.

What is a pattern you might ask? Any obstacle, hardship or adverse
encounter that continually shows up in our lives signifies a pattern.
Clearly the pattern continues in our lives until it's addressed.
Our patterns show up everywhere in our lives — at work, at home,
in our relationships with lovers, colleagues, family, friends and strangers.
Patterns are highlighted over and over in our lives until we work through them.
If we do not catch the pattern, it will undoubtedly repeat again,
but with a new situation and a new cast of characters.

Your work is to wake up to the patterns,
catch them and heal them so that you can be freed of them.
Once you wake up and apply a certain degree of conscious awareness
to your life, your life changes.
Patterns are meant to be addressed and worked through,
not experienced over and over again.

The next time you find yourself in a tough spot, stop and ask yourself if
there is a pattern here that you are not seeing.
Has something similar happened before?
Once you catch the pattern, you can choose to show up differently and
make a new decision that will change your outcome.
As long as you stay stuck repeating negative patterns of behavior,
you keep yourself back in life.
Patterns keep you stuck. Healing the patterns set you free.
Where do you want to be?

Think Before You Act

... you can't take it back.

Believe it or not, all words and actions have consequences,
some more severe than others.
Sometimes when we are out of balance in our lives,
we make impulsive decisions that may affect our futures.
These impulsive decisions are made simply with the intent to make us feel
better in the moment and NOT made for our highest good.

Life is meant to be led one step at a time.
Every emotion is meant to be felt and dealt with, not run from.
*If you are making an impulsive decision to feel better in the moment and run from
your pain, it will catch up with you.*
You cannot run from yourself and life offers us no "quick fixes,"
that is for sure.

Slow down, take life one step at a time.
Ask yourself before you make ANY decision,
"Is this decision going to bring me to where I want to be in my life" OR
"Is it going to sabotage my job, my love, or my relations with friends and
family?" Once we slow down and process the implications of our actions,
we may find that we are in a better place to make a different decision.

It is in a calm and centered space that we find the ability to NOT
react hastily and make a decision we may later regret.
Life is too short to impulsively throw it away on a bad decision.
No one needs to look back and regret something they have done.
Stop. Slow down. Be in the moment and think before you act.
I promise you, if you live your life from this centered space,
you will always make an informed decision, NOT an impulsive one.
We want to own our lives, not regret them.

You're Never a Victim Of Your Life

... you're only a victim of your CHOICES.

So if you are unhappy with any area of your life,
MAKE ANOTHER CHOICE. It's as simple as that.

We get stuck in negative patterns where we think that we are being held
back from success or abundance, or held back from love, or
we feel stuck and treated unfairly in our lives when in reality
we are just reaping the ramifications of our own choices.

No one is making you do anything.

No one is keeping you somewhere you do not want to be.

No one is making life difficult for you but YOU.

If you choose to give your power over to anyone or to any situation to
allow yourself to feel broken and disempowered then realize that
that is a CHOICE. No one has any power over you unless
you give it to them. You have a choice every day as to how you are going
to show up in life and what kind of day you are going to make of it.
Remember *the quality of your life is in direct response to the choices you make.*
If you want a better life, seek ways to improve upon your circumstances.
Make different choices than the ones that have led you to where you are.

Life is too short to bemoan your fate and accept less than desirable outcomes.
It is up to you to recognize that the way you have conducted your life
thus far is not working for you and be open enough to
bring about the change you truly want and deserve.
Are you ready to make another choice?
The rest of your life is contingent on it.

Chapter 4

Relationships

Once you know who you are and
you learn to love and value yourself AND
you have learned the rules of the game of life,
you are ready to interact whole-heartedly in
REAL relationships.

We only know who we are "in relation"
to other human beings
which is why our romantic relationships
tend to be the most challenging.

Relationships are where we do the most growth in our lives.
It's where we really learn who we are and
how we show up in life.

Relationships are never easy; they were never meant to be,
but they offer the most rewarding aspects of our life here on earth.
After all, you only know who you are in life
when you learn who you are not.

Chapter 4

Relationships

My life has been a personal journey into understanding relationships and the significance they hold in our lives. Along my path, I have learned that the most significant relationship we can ever have in our life is the relationship with our own SELF.

I personally have lost many relationships in my life because I had lost my ability to love myself first and put my needs first. I am a loving person and I give too much to others in all my relationships. One of my life lessons is to learn to not prioritize others' needs ahead of my own. It took me awhile to understand this (and in some ways I am still challenged by it).

I do have abandonment issues, and interestingly enough, they are not even from this lifetime. And so despite the fact that I am feeling uncomfortable in a relationship (a clear sign that your needs are not being met), I stay with it and try to give more to my partner to help find that balance. I find that I inadvertently do the work for both of us. I try to carry the load of the entire relationship and then I get resentful and lash out at them out of frustration for doing so. But how can I be upset with them for doing the work for both of us when I set it up that way? Clearly if I was looking for a different outcome, I should have approached the relationship differently and planted different seeds – seeds of loving myself and not accepting bulls--- from them upfront. But unfortunately, I stay in it and try to rectify the issues of being abandoned lifetimes earlier.

So, what happens? I get tested with each relationship. I get thrown a guy who seems perfect on paper, and trust me, they are all pretty perfect on paper! But they are never perfect in the way they show up (or don't show up) for me. That is the common denominator for me. These men are all beautiful souls (inside and out) and filled with potential. Because I am clairsentient, I can feel their hearts and their potential, and I fall in love with that potential even though it is not necessarily how they are showing up for me. I wait. I wait and I wait. I wait for them to wake up and realize that all the spiritual knowledge and friendship and professional support I have given them is worthy of a healthy relationship. And because I have put their needs, their neuroses, their values and their schedules ahead of my own, I lose. Why? Because I have forgotten that the only relationship that matters and the only relationship that I am supposed to be honoring in my life is my relationship to myself.

Inevitably, the relationship ends, because I finally walk away from it (broken hearted and confused), but in reality, they had emotionally left me months before.

Chapter 4

Relationships

I should also say that these men are all common in their attachment to me – they need my insights/inspiration, my professional help, my spiritual guidance and my friendship/support, but are always unwilling to give in return. They are also very reluctant to let me go, which makes it hard on me when they try to manipulate me into staying a bit longer to satisfy whatever need they have in that moment. Even when they are involved with other women, they still do not want to cut the cord with me! And because I generally want to help them be better and help advance them and their careers, I stay in an unhealthy place in support of them.

They also tend to be narcissistic, self-centered, emotionally immature and very much grounded in their egos. Apparently, as I have been told by my spiritual teachers, I am a catalyst for their evolution and growth. They are attracted to "my light" and they meet me at a time in their life when they really want to make change. They then get to a testing point where they can either choose to do the work inwardly (spiritually change and grow by learning about themselves and owning their behaviors) or they can choose to continue focusing externally/superficially (on the ego and the material world which masks their internal dialogue). Yup, it's always the same story; I am a mirror to them, and through me they see that they still have work to do on themselves and I am reminder of that. And let's face it, no one wants to be reminded of that. It is much easier, happier and "better" to be involved with people who admire, respect and are in awe of you. But that only gets you so far in life. Eventually your work will catch up with you and, as we will discuss in this book, the longer it takes you to get your lessons, the harder they get for you. It's part of life.

Now I will say that these men are all very strong and accomplished in their own ways and deserve to be admired and appreciated for all that they do, but in my reality, I am unimpressed by ego achievements (fame, fortune, materiality). I am impressed with people who inspire ME to want to be a better person. And these men DO want to put good out into the world and they ARE charitable to some degree, but they have a very strong ego need to be seen doing that and be acknowledged for their efforts. I can smell ego a mile away, and so these men inevitably end up feeling judged by me. They feel "less than" somehow because they have a need to have their egos elevated and therefore they opt for something "easier, lighter, happier." They emotionally withdraw and run out the door either by cheating and destroying a committed relationship with me, or they decide they want to continue dating other

Chapter 4

Relationships

people because they feel it is too much work to be involved with me – which is ironic because I am the one who does everything to keep it together! I make these men better men for other women (which is my spiritual contract with them) and they destroy me emotionally, but again, I set it up that way. So who's to blame here?

What's the lesson, you might ask? My work is to find the balance in committed relationships; not give everything over to them, not try to do all the work in the relationship to keep it going, but to love myself enough to ask for more from the relationship and when I do not get it, to love myself enough to walk out the door without losing myself in the process. And most importantly to remember that it's not my job to fix or save anyone from themselves.

Am I there yet? Let's just say that with each passing relationship, I learn more and more about myself and my patterns. Relationships are mirrors to us, and with each mirror we do not always like what we see, but when we can focus on that reflection, we can decide how to make it work better for us.

The following essays are my foundational teachings (derived from my personal experience and from that of my teachers) on what it takes to be in healthy, happy relationship with yourself and with all others – not just romantic relationships. I hope they help to inspire you along your journey in all your relationships.

If You Are In It, Be In It

... otherwise get OUT of it.

There's NO in between.
This is especially true of our romantic relationships.
If you are in one, BE IN IT and make it work, otherwise,
get out of it and move on.

Complaining about your relationship will not make it better.
Staying and cheating does not make it better.
Wishing you were with someone else will not make it better.
Trying to change that person will not make it better.

*The only thing that will make it better is a genuine
commitment to healing by BOTH parties.*
There are 2 people in the relationship and
BOTH have to commit to working on it.

If both parties are NOT willing, there isn't any hope. Time to leave.

Don't kid yourself. Don't hold on and hope things will change.
Change ONLY happens when both parties work together.
Where is your relationship?
Can the other person be as committed as you are to healing?
If not, you may have to look elsewhere.

Having history together does not make a relationship work.
Having a genuine interest in securing a happy tomorrow will.
It is always your choice. But if you choose to be in it, BE IN IT and get
that person to work with you.
Don't accept no for an answer.
If you find the answer is still no, time to make a gracious exit.
Don't let the memories keep you stuck.
Your life is ahead of you and if that person
cannot/will not work WITH YOU, don't even look back.
Run towards a happier tomorrow.

Growing Together, Growing Apart

... which do you prefer?

It's human nature to continue to grow throughout your lifetime.

And when we are in a relationship with someone, we have a choice, we can either *grow with them or we can grow apart from them, but we will continue to grow regardless*. It is the way the universe works.

The question remains: how do you want to grow in your relationship?

The hope is that the relationship you choose supports your growth and the direction you want to move into in your life. But that isn't always the case. Sometimes we choose partners for other reasons only to find out after a period of time that we no longer have anything in common and our desires/passions have waned.

That doesn't mean that someone has to be exactly like you but it does mean that they have to be able to push you/challenge you in new ways to grow and expand your mind. Mutual respect and admiration will keep the two of you learning about each other and interested in each other's journey. *If you are on different paths and you are NOT interested in each other's journey, nor is there any shared journey, it will NEVER last.* Clearly, you are growing apart.

Having said that, growing together isn't necessarily easy. *Don't look for the easy way out. Easy is just that: EASY. It doesn't mean better.* And easy will more often than not turn into boring very quickly.

A better relationship is generally a bit more challenging. A better relationship should *inspire* you but at the same time should *challenge* you to pick it up a bit. It keeps you on your toes and keeps you growing and evolving. This dynamism will never tire and never get boring.

In any relationship it is important to know who you are. Know what's important to you and pick relationships that can support and nurture you on that journey.

Don't kid yourself – you will grow regardless, so it's best to be conscious of the tide you are riding before you find yourself in a place you didn't mean to get to. Do you want to grow together or grow apart? The choice is always yours. Choose wisely.

Pack Your Bags Lightly

... you take it all with you.

It is human nature to carry your bags with you. All of them.
We all carry heavy burdens of issues – packed up discreetly or not so discreetly
as our "baggage." We insist on carting this baggage around with us
into every new relationship, job and situation.

We try and show up as the best version of ourselves,
yet we will not let go of our bags.
We stand smiling at the front door while we are invited in by our host
and instead of discreetly storing our bags away in the guest closet until it
is time to unpack them, we find ourselves running into our host's main
room and exploding open our bags like a crazy person –
exposing the most intimate parts of ourselves at very inopportune times.
Why do we do this?

In life, there is a big difference between being open/vulnerable and
being needy/unconscious. You always want to be yourself and be genuine
but at the same time, it is important that you are conscious.
It is important that you realize everything that you have packed into your
bags and recognize it is yours when it rears its ugly head out of the baggage.
Never confuse its contents with those of your host.
In other words: *own what is yours and give the rest back.*

You have a lifetime to sort through your baggage. Try and streamline it –
deal with your issues and evolve onwards. You will blame people less, resent people less,
distrust people less and grow consciously into the being you were meant to.
Life gets easier for you and people find it easier to be around you.

Do the work – *lessen your load, you do not need to throw your dirty laundry all over
your partner's living room in order to be seen and heard.*
There is a better way to show up. Pack your bags lightly;
the soul is eternal and your baggage is your load to carry
lifetime after lifetime.
How heavy are your bags? It might be time to lighten your load.

When People Get Stuck In Their Stories

... they cannot hear you.

They only hear what they want to hear or what they've been conditioned to
hear. But regardless, when they are stuck in their own story,
they won't be able to hear you.

We all have these scripts that run inside our heads about who we are and
how we show up in life. And just for the record,
they are generally not very accurate.
They tend to be the *limiting, self-destructive scripts that keep us from greatness
and/or keep us from learning how to truly connect with others.*

It takes a very open minded and balanced being to be open enough/
aware enough to hear the constructive comments of others and be able
to distinguish them from the deconstructive comments.
*An open minded being doesn't shut down when faced with constructive criticism; they
embrace it and seek to grow and evolve with it.*
Ask yourself if you are able to find constructive criticism in people's
words or if you just shut down when you hear things you don't like?

On the flip side, have you tried to say something to someone you love
and they just don't get it? Don't make yourself crazy.
You can't change people's stories for them; it's not your place to do so.
They live them everyday. They need them to exist.
It's not your job to fix anyone or save them from themselves.
*If they cannot hear what you are saying to them, it isn't time for them to do that work
with you.* Back off and save your breath.
Put your energy back into yourself. Don't take it personally.
Not everyone is able and ready to rewrite their stories.
Some prefer to relive them over and over again because
it is easier than trying to grow into new and unchartered territory.

Are you stuck in your story? Want to be free?
Learn to let go of what you think defines you and open up to a new way of being.
Life is too short to keep yourself stuck. If you stay stuck in your story,
you will never hear anyone and chances are there is a newer and much
better story out there for you. It might be time to go out and find it. 63

When People Tell You Who They Are

... believe them.

So often we want to believe in the good of others.
We want to give them the benefit of the doubt.
We see so much potential in them – so much so that we are willing to
overlook anything to the contrary.
We make excuses for people; we turn a cheek to pain and
betrayal in hopes that it will never happen again.
We assure ourselves that every indignation is a one-off –
"They are just having a bad day," we tell ourselves.

Now understand that it is a great gift to be able to believe in people and
see their hearts… to believe in them and see what no one else sees. But at
the same time, *it is a great curse to ignore what is right in front of you.*

When people tell you (by way of showing you) who they are, BELIEVE them. Talk
(and email) is very cheap. We use vocabulary as manipulation. Actions are
the most telling. When you enter that new relationship,
the first time that person crosses your boundaries,
make a note – this is who they are. They may not say as such,
but their actions tell you everything you need to know.
When they offer bad behavior upfront, do not believe in their potential to change.
Do not think that you are an exception to the rule, that you will somehow
change them, that you will somehow convert them into
a better version of themselves.
It never works.

In reality people do not change, and it is wrong of you to expect that they will.
People can want to change and can even go through the motions of
trying to change, but at its essence level, change is extremely difficult –
especially the older we get and the less disciplined we are.
If you want a healthy relationship, be a good "listener" and hear what is
actually being "said" to you.
When people tell you who they are, believe them.

When People Walk Away

... let them go.

As humans we have a very hard time letting go, but it's important to
remember that *not everyone is supposed to be in your life forever.*
People filter in and out of your life during certain times to fulfill certain
roles and when those roles are fulfilled, they are free to move on.

Some people in our lives are like the limbs of a tree;
they grow with the tree and they weather the storm with the tree.
And some people are like the leaves; they come in during a season of
your life to change you, support you or inspire you and then they move on.
It is important to be able to distinguish who is a limb and who is a leaf in your life.
Once you identify your limbs, it is much easier to let the leaves fall to the
wayside. A tree cannot hold onto its leaves; when it is time,
they will organically wither and die off – it is a natural cycle of life.
Why would we think relationships would be any different?

Anyone who walks away without a fight was never going to stay for the long haul.

Bless those leaves as they fall from your life and focus on the limbs of
your tree, they are always there to support you.
There will always be new leaves again in the springtime and
the cycle will always repeat.
Learn who your limbs are and let the leaves go,
they were only there for a season of your life and that season has gone.

When a Relationship Ends

... you are supposed to MOVE ON.

It doesn't matter how or why it ends, it only matters that
you acknowledge the ending and take the learning with you.

Relationships are opportunities for us to grow and learn.
When you learn what you have needed to learn from each other, then the relationship ends.
It is time to start a new chapter to practice your learning in a new situation.

Now, that does NOT mean that the relationship will never come back to
you in a newer, healed form later on.
But it does tell you that *for now, your work with each other is complete.*

Problems arise when we do not let go of the relationship, but hold on out
of fear of need or fear of being alone.
*When you hold on too long, it only creates frustration, pain and stagnation,
and ultimately will keep all happiness and growth from you.*

When a relationship ends, the most important thing you can do is to be
strong and learn to graciously accept the new changes.
Trust in the universe to bring you to where you need to be.
If your relationship was not meant to end, it wouldn't be ending.
If it is ending, it is because it is time for it to do so.

Don't drive your relationship into the ground by holding on too long.
Everything happens for a reason and despite the fact that you may feel it
is not yet time for your relationship to be ending,
the universe may just have other plans for you.
Learn to trust and *learn to find the "good" in "goodbye,"*
for it is ALWAYS there.

Need Is Never Love

... it is NEED.

Only love is love.

But we confuse the two. We get into situations where we think because
we love someone that we NEED them in order to feel whole.
*If you are needing someone to be something or do something for you to feel whole, then
realize that that is never love – it is in fact only need.*

Need is what we need to learn to give to ourselves.
Once we take care of our own needs, then real love follows.
But we have a habit of looking for love and then putting our needs
on that love as if it is our love's responsibility
to fix us or save us from ourselves.

*It is no one else's responsibility to give you what you NEED.
It is your responsibility to take care of your own needs and make sure
you always have what you need in order to feel whole in yourself.*
When you can manage your needs effectively, real love has the opportunity
to complement you, not complete you.
*When you manage your needs, you find that the love you attract is always able to give
you what you need, because you have given it to yourself first.*

For example, if you need someone to provide for you,
learn to provide for yourself.
If you need someone to see you as successful, find success in yourself.
If you need someone to see you as beautiful, see the beauty in yourself.

Once you have honored those needs in yourself, real love will be able to
provide you with so much more richness and happiness.

So remember, *need is need – it is never love.*
Real love is the ability to give yourself what you need in order to feel whole.
All you need is love – real love to be whole and it starts with loving yourself.

You Can't Fix People

... you can only fix yourself.

You are not responsible for anyone.
You cannot save them from themselves. It is simply not your work.
This makes things challenging for us
when we are involved with people who may need a bit of guidance.
It's human nature to want to help and it's also human nature to want
people *to act in a way that makes you happy, but life doesn't work that way.*
You have to let people be who they are and if who they are doesn't work for you,
it might be time to make a different choice.

The road to misery is paved with those who have set up
unrealistic expectations of their partners or what's worse,
have tried to change their partner's behavior outright.
When people tell you who they are, BELIEVE THEM and don't spend time
trying to change them. It doesn't work.
It only succeeds in frustrating you and
depleting you of your positive energy and life force.

Everyone has their own work to do.
Yours is to focus on your life lessons and spend less time
trying to improve upon others' lessons.
If you try to do the work for others, not only will you exhaust yourself
and be left feeling very resentful, but you will disempower them to do
their own work and they will only end up shutting down to you.
What you try to fix and save will surely backfire on you.

If you truly want to "fix" people and make them into
"better versions of themselves,"
inspire them to do the work themselves.
You do this by being the best version of who you are every day –
loving yourself and making the highest choice for yourself
even if it means walking away from less than desired behavior.
Set an example of integrity for them to follow.
This also means refraining from complaining, whining and launching
frontal attacks when you are not getting your way, or worse,
shutting down and disengaging when you don't want to deal.
These are childish tactics that never yield the benefit sought.

Don't expect people to be OTHER than who they are.
Don't kid yourself into thinking they will change.
Don't buy into the potential you see in them.
Accept them for who they are and what they are willing to give you OR
DON'T. *Life is too short to spend your time doing others' work.*
It's not yours to do and they will not appreciate it.
Do the math; you are the one who loses.
Learn to love yourself enough to let people
simply be who they are.

Ask And You Will Receive

... don't ask, and you will surely never get.

Translation... *we do NOT get what we do NOT ask for.*
It is as simple as that.

So often we make concessions for others' bad behavior.
Maybe we do not want to rock the boat with a boss or employee?
Maybe we are too afraid to speak our minds with our significant other or friend?
You only get what you need by putting it out there.
In my experience, people are not mind-readers.
If their behavior is not yielding the results you require
to be in a given partnership, then you have a responsibility to yourself
to ask for what it is you need.

Many of us tend to not speak up for fear of being rejected.
We prefer to put other people's happiness and comfort levels ahead of our own.
It seems a safer bet than to rock the boat and risk potential consequences.
But if you take a back seat to others' happiness, you will never be in the
driver seat of your own life, and will always be at the mercy of other
people's mood swings and outbursts. If you value yourself and your
happiness and well-being, you will always put your needs front and center.
*After all, it is only when you give the oxygen mask to yourself that
you have enough to give to those you love.*

Getting what you want in life starts with loving yourself and knowing you
deserve better than what you are currently receiving.
If you do not speak out, not only do you lose by not receiving what you
deeply desire and deserve, but your partner loses a valuable opportunity
to grow in relationship to you. Learning and evolving works both ways.
*When we deprive ourselves of what we need, generally we deprive others of the opportunity
to truly know us and learn to give us what we actually need.*
It is a lose-lose for both parties.

When you choose you, everyone wins. Put your needs first,
ask for what you deserve, do not accept less and watch the scales re-balance.
We do not get what we do not ask for. What are you holding out for?

Chapter 5

Letting Go

It's human nature to hold onto people and situations
that have outlived their usefulness in our lives.
But holding on keeps us locked in the past.
As humans, our work is to evolve and move forward and
not look back.

Your past is your past for a reason.
If it was meant to be in your present, it would be standing
right in front of you, and if it is meant to be part of your future,
it will come back when it is time.

Let go of what is not working in your life so you can make
room for what will.
You can never lose what is real for you.
If it is real, it will always come back on schedule.
So learn to lose what doesn't work
so you can win what will.

Chapter 5

Letting Go

Letting go is tough for most people, and it has definitely been one of my greatest hardships in this lifetime. I tend to see the potential in people and I believe in them, even though they may not always show up as the ideal version of themselves.

I tend to give people the benefit of the doubt that they are "having a bad day/week/month/year." I wait and wait for them to show up as the beings I know they are in their heart. But that never serves me. It always backfires on me because I wait too long for them to become something they have decided NOT to become. And since I wait too long, I generally manage to stress the relationship with my own frustrations that they are not living up to the person I know they could be. I end up inadvertently driving the relationship into the ground under the guise of trying to help them. Now, I will not take on all the responsibility, as they have had their part in this as well, but I will accept the fact that I ALWAYS hold on too long. My work is to let go as soon as I realize that the relationship is not heading in the direction that suits both our needs, instead of waiting around for that person to decide to grow into the being I know they can be. Being able to "see" people is definitely a mixed blessing for me because it always confuses me when they show up differently from who I know they can be. But regardless, my work is to learn to more quickly let go of people and situations that are not serving me/my needs and to not wait around optimistically hoping that the situation will change.

The following essays give me solace when I know it's time to end something that is not working in my life, and I hope they can do the same for you.

Staying Too Long

... makes you miss your stop.

Sometimes we stay too long in spaces we shouldn't –
spaces such as dead-end jobs and dead-end relationships.
We stay hoping somehow we can transform them into being
what we need them to be.
Staying too long doesn't remedy a bad situation; it makes it worse.
It overstays your welcome and drains the situation or rather,
runs it into the ground.

Be honest with yourself.
Are you staying because it is what you really want and deserve,
or are you staying for some other reason based out of fear such as,
"I don't think I can do better," or, "There aren't any other opportunities
out there for me," or, "I will never be able to do what I really want."

Don't stay too long in spaces that are not working for you.
Yours is not to force fit them to meet your needs.
*Yours is to be strong enough to be able to discern what is best for you and
for your growth and let the rest fall by the wayside.*

Staying too long makes you miss your stop.
Life is like a train ride from New York City to Boston.
You will always get to your final destination in life; it is your destiny.
You will reach Boston one way or another.
But it is your choice as to whether or not you will enjoy the journey along the way.
That journey has some beautiful shoreline along Connecticut.
*If you stay too long at certain stops, you will miss the beautiful views and experiences
that that journey has to offer.*

Don't try and hold the doors open and stay in the station.
Let the doors close. Let yourself get to the next stop and get out and take
a look around. Life is too short to stay at one stop for too long.
There is a whole coastline out there for you to explore.
Give yourself the chance to have some great experiences and when they
have served their purpose, be strong enough to let them leave your life.
On to the next stop...

Releasing Your Grip

... allows things to breathe.

Trying to hyper-control situations strangle-holds them.

We hold so tightly to what it is we think is right for us.
In fact, we continually push our agendas forward even in the face of
adversity. But to what end? Where do we stop and realize that
resistance is a form of protection.
If you are finding it hard to continue on in a given direction,
it might be because you are not meant to.
Resistance is a universal sign to back off.
There is something there that you might not be seeing.

We are conditioned to think that if we work hard enough and push hard
enough that we can alter any situation to our advantage,
but that is using force to drive your life.
A better way of living your life is to STOP pushing when you hit a wall and step back.
Give yourself some space and time to breathe and allow what is meant to
make its way to you, to get to you.
Your future might need a bit of course correction.

Your life is divine. There is an order to it.
There is fate and destiny already in place.
You can always use your free will to alter any and all of it, but note that
you will absolutely encounter resistance if you are pushing towards the wrong conclusion.
Take that as a sign to stop exhausting yourself. Take that step back so you
can see more clearly. *That step back will free up the energy to allow
what is really meant for you to catch up with you.*
Time and space is the ultimate neutralizer.

You want to learn to breathe your way through your life.
Controlling doesn't secure your future; allowing does. When you are ready to release
your grip on what you thought you wanted/needed,
you will be able to make room for something even more beautiful.
Clarity comes from releasing your grip, letting go of control and learning
to trust in the process of your life to bring you to exactly where you need to be.

Where else would you want to go?

Learn To Let It Pass Through You

... not take you down.

What you attach to becomes yours but what you detach from
NEVER impacts you.

You have a choice every day as to what you will allow to affect you.
If something in your life is upsetting you, don't fight it, let it pass through you.
When you fight/resist something, you give it life and validity.
But when you detach from it, you diffuse its energy and
it no longer has such control over you.

Life gets hard when you carry burdens that you don't need to carry.
If you don't want it in your life, don't give it any attention.
Learn to let it pass through you, don't attach to it and
you will disarm the situation completely.
What was meant to be a full out drama will just barely irritate you.

By yielding to the storm, a blade of grass will allow the storm to pass
right through it, whereas the old, stubborn tree will be snapped in half if
it does not yield to those winds.
As in all negative situations, learn to let it pass through you and
you will be the one left standing when the sun comes out again.

Life is too short to attach to every drama that comes your way.
Don't bother resisting the negativity; you will only succeed in feeding it.
You want a better life? Learn to let things pass through you.
Only accept the situations that you want to engage in and
let the rest fall to the wayside.

Lose What Doesn't Work

... to make room for what will.

We have a tendency to hold onto things and situations in our lives that do NOT work. It is almost as if we think that by holding tighter to what isn't working that it will all of a sudden somehow become what we need? But this never happens.

In life we need space to create what we want/need and
when that space is filled up with what isn't working,
it takes up valuable real estate and tells the universe that
we do NOT want better.

You have to free yourself of what is not working
so you can fill the space with what will work.
Trying to force something to work NEVER makes it work.
Taking a step back and giving the situation the space to breathe
will allow the energies to re-align and bring about the highest outcome
for all involved.

Sometimes in life *you have to lose to win.*
Riding a broken bike will never win you the bike-a-thon, but retiring the
bike to the bike shop for a period of time will guarantee that
you are ready to get back behind the starting line of the next one.

Life is too short to hold onto what doesn't work for you.
Let it go and love yourself enough to ask for better.
Losing is the great arbiter of justice.
By losing it all, you have half a chance of finding what will work better for you.
Losing is definitely the winning strategy.
Be happy to lose!

Don't Look Back

... you are not going that way.

Referencing the past keeps you stuck in it.
In life, *moving on is the name of the game.*
Never do we want to look back for the answers.
Looking back will never help you move forward. It just never will.

Whatever challenge you have come through needs to stay in the past,
whether it be a break-up, divorce, bankruptcy, getting fired, etc...
Challenges are meant to be overcome and moved beyond.
Don't dwell on the negativity.
Don't allow feelings of guilt, regret or pain
keep you stuck in a cycle of decreasing self-worth.

Now, this does not mean ignore your weaknesses and
pretend your issues are not yours.
It simply means when dealing with memories of the past,
it is critical that *you get the lesson and get out.*
Don't continue to relive the situation and
the emotions in your mind over and over again.
Learn what you need to learn and shut it down.
Move forward with those lessons and make positive change in your life.

Carrying the heavy burden of those past memories only drags you down
and slows your growth.
It keeps you locked in the past and keeps it alive in your heart.

Your past is your past for a reason. If it was supposed to be in your present,
it would be standing right in front of you and
if it is supposed to be in your future, it will catch up with you when it is time.
But looking back at it only keeps you stuck and
doesn't allow you to get on with your life.
Keep walking. If your past is meant to be with you,
it will come and find you when the time is right.
Never look back for the answers... only look ahead.
Your life is ahead of you, not behind you.

Nothing Ever Leaves Your Life

... until it has taught you what you need to know.

People and situations come in and out of our lives to teach us something.
It is a part of life. The true learning comes from recognizing that
if someone or something has left your life, it is because it was time for it to do so.
Once we learn the lessons we move on to a much higher playing field.

Trouble begins when we are reluctant to let go of what
we know is not serving us (toxic job, relationship, etc.). It is up to you to
recognize when a person or situation has outlived its purpose and let it go.
You know you are holding on too long when the situation becomes un-
compromising, frustrating and you are beating your head on a wall over
and over again with no new result.
*You can hold onto that old lesson but doing so will assure you of
reliving that lesson over and over again.*
But we rarely acknowledge this pattern in ourselves.
Instead we prefer to hold on and hope the situation
will change in our favor, but it never does.

What's worse with holding on to old lessons is that you can only hold
onto them for so long before they get ripped away from you and
you are you left with nothing but a sense of loss and abandonment.
*The universe will eventually clear the decks and take away
what you were not strong enough to do yourself.*

Why keep yourself back? Recognize when you get the lesson and be
strong enough to extract yourself from the negative pattern.
Invite change and new life in. You cannot hold onto your
"accomplishments" forever; eventually it is time to evolve them and
encourage yourself to grow past them.
This is how we grow.
*You cannot lose what is real for you; if it leaves your life,
it is because you are meant to grow beyond it.*

Letting Go Of The Old

... is the only way to move forward into the new

Somehow we think that keeping the old
will enable us to open the door to the new. It never does.
When a person or a situation has outlived its purpose,
it is important to close the door on the old, so that you can create SPACE for the new.

Holding onto what does not serve you does not all of a sudden change.
If you decide to pack up what didn't work for you this year and sling it
over your shoulder and haul it into next year,
you will get the same nonsense in that next year.
If it didn't work for you then, I promise you, it will not all of a sudden work now.

Why burden yourself with what you know does not make you happy?
When you learn to cut ties to the past and open up to a bright new future,
you are creating space for the new future to come in.
But when you hold onto what does not work for you,
it is as if you are telling the universe you are content and
you do not need something new.
Look at it this way: if your glass is full of dirty water that you cannot
drink, in essence, you are telling the universe that you do not need a refill
of fresh water. But in actuality, you are dying of thirst.
Pour out the dirty water and allow yourself
to be filled with what you truly want and desire in life.

You cannot create change if there is no space.
Don't spend your life being "full" with what is making you unhappy.
Be strong and allow yourself the opportunity
to throw out the old and make room for the new.
The rest of your life awaits.
What are you waiting for?

Moving On

... is truly the purpose of life.

But unfortunately we never see it that way.
We get caught up in the daily dramas of life and
tend to allow our challenges to overwhelm us and sometimes win over us.

Life is filled with challenges.
Yours is to NOT give in to the challenges, yours is to

FACE them.

RISE ABOVE them.

GROW from them.

and make yourself BETTER because of them.

No one said life was going to be easy. If you wanted easy,
you wouldn't have chosen this life. You are here because
you chose to evolve. So here is where the work begins.

Don't spend your life hiding under rocks from those challenges.
Those challenges represent your life lessons. They are there for a reason.
They are there to test your reserve and your fortitude.
They are there to bring up your darkest fears and insecurities.
They are there to force you to look into the mirror and see who you really are.
You really learn who you are once you have overcome
a huge obstacle in your life.
We say it is "character building."

Sometimes your challenges can drop you to your knees
but again, yours is not to lie down and sulk,
yours is to get right back up and keep walking.
Moving on is the name of the game.
That is the only way you can transform the lesson.
Do you want to live your life like a coward hiding under a rock or
do you want to meet those challenges face-on screaming
"Give me your best shot!".
Who you are is always greater than your lessons. Always.
Who you are will always persevere against adversity and
all challenges but you must believe in yourself for it to be so.

Don't decide to roll over and feign death –
you cannot hide from your challenges. You can buy yourself time –
maybe a year or two –
but that challenge will always come back with a vengeance,
and when it does, *the lesson always gets harder.*

Stand up to your challenges and transform them.
Move on with your life. Make your life better because of what you have gone through.
The rest of your life awaits and it is filled with
many rich rewards for all your bravery.

Bend Don't Break

...learn to be flexible.

Learn to let things wash over you.

When we try to resist hardship, change, pain or heartbreak,
we make it harder then it needs to be.
Don't fight the experience; learn to let it wash over you and leave you.

Many of us attach to the hardship; we personalize it and over-dramatize it
and create bigger obstacles that need to be surmounted.
Negative energy builds upon itself.
If you want to create a monster, you can.
What you resist persists, but what you learn to look at disappears.

Be flexible, learn to navigate life with ease and grace no matter what is going on
around you and you will ALWAYS have a better result.
The slight and fragile blade of grass is still standing after a great storm,
but the tall, resistant oak tree will be snapped in half.
Strength does not guarantee success but the ability to yield to trouble
allows you more options for survival.
In the middle of the storm, bending and yielding buys you time
until the sun comes out. If you resist,
you will always be snapped in half... and Game Over.

Let each storm pass through you, and as it does,
it will teach you something about yourself.
It changes you and you find that
you truly learn how to weather the storm.
In life, don't resist the inevitable... power through it,
allow it to pass through you over and over again until the storm stops.
When all is said and done,
you will be the one left standing.

Chapter 6

Change

No one likes it, but we all have to do it.

Change is an integral part of living life on Earth.
Avoiding change only keeps you locked in unhappy spaces.
Fear of the unknown is nothing compared to
the fear of NOT growing.
Being stuck and stagnant creates more problems
than marching into the unknown.

At least by moving forward, you are guaranteed to reach
the sunshine versus sitting out on the lawn in the rainstorm.
That only gets you wet.

Change is the way we grow and evolve.
Staying stuck is the way we shrink from our greatness.
Which direction are you headed?

Chapter 6

Change

Change scares us. No one likes it. I will say though that it is only through change that we can grow and become the beautiful beings we were meant to become. No one wants to be at the same place they were in high school, do they? There are many more mountains to climb and experiences to have.

I have watched myself grow leaps and bounds through periods of change. Those transitional periods are the periods where we transform ourselves from caterpillars into beautiful butterflies. Those transitional periods are never easy; in fact, they are purposely disorientating and frightening, but they yield the most amazing results. In just five years, I went from being a creative director at a national design magazine to being a very successful life coach, nutritionist, yoga teacher, blogger, and author whose work centers on helping inspire positive change in the lives of others. None of that would have happened had I not open up to the prospect of change, as scary as it was for me. It was all an offer for me, if I were just to jump in and seize it. My dad always told me, *"never regret the things you do in life; only regret the things that you don't do."* There is an inherent platform for change here. That statement has helped set me up on a journey of change throughout my life. It has enabled me to take chances where normally I might not.

Thanks to my dad, I have no regrets in my life. I have accepted change each time it has come knocking at my door. It has always brought me down different paths and has helped me to evolve into the teacher I have become today. Change makes you better. Without change, I would have never had the opportunity to experience who I really am. I might still be sitting at my desk on Central Park staring at the trees wondering what I was meant to do with my life. When change comes knocking, you'd best answer the door. The rest of your life awaits on the other side.

The following essays have given me the strength to open up to all facets of change in my own life. They have reminded me that *you can never lose by moving forward and evolving,* and that the only loss is in staying still. I hope that they give you the same encouragement and support for the periods of change in your life.

Staying Never Gets You Anywhere

... it keeps you in the same place.

Only movement initiates action.

Whatever changes you would like to make in your life require some type
of movement, strategic movement NOT "busy" movement.
Strategic movement has the intention of bringing about change.
Busy movement is activity that uses your energy but
doesn't bring about the desired result (e.g. being too busy at work to have
the time to look for a new job or spending your time trying
to fix a relationship when the other person is doing nothing).

Strategic movement is movement to initiate change, NOT propagate the same stasis.
Be honest with yourself and ask yourself if you see your actions
as helping you move forward or keeping you stuck in your own patterns.

It's very simple: if you are standing still, you cannot move forward.
And if you are looking behind you, you cannot move forward.
You can only move forward by making the extreme effort to do so.

We keep ourselves back in life by not allowing ourselves to move forward,
but instead, we stand still and complain about the situation.
*Staying in the situation and bemoaning it
will only charge it with more negativity and unhappiness.*

Time to break the cycle. *Staying never gets you anywhere.*
*If you want to move forward, you have to bring in a type of strategic movement or
change that will NOT allow you to look back at your past,
but push you forward into your dreams.*
Nothing else will do.

Waiting For Your Life To Come Together

... assures that it never will.

Nothing ever comes from inactivity.
The universe does not understand inactivity.
A body in motion must always stay in motion if it is to go anywhere.
A body at rest, by definition, never moves forward.

If you are waiting for your life to just come together on its own,
without your direction, or inspiration or even intuitive guidance,
you will be waiting a very long time.
You must be an active participant in your life in order to manifest what you are seeking.
This means you need to show initiative to create any newness in your life.
You need to get up out of the place that is not working for you
in order to start the wheels of change.

*There is always a destiny in place for you, but it requires that
you WALK your path of destiny.*
Destiny will not just deliver life to you.
It assumes that you are living your life and moving
through your experiences for better or worse.
This activity will bring you to the next phase of your life on schedule.
But to fight the flow of life by giving up and staying still and stagnant
is to throw away the gift that you were given.

Waiting for your life to come together is a means of passive self-sabotage
and it usually happens when someone has been relatively traumatized by a
situation and they decide it's better to take no action
then to risk possible wrong action.
The only wrong action in life is inaction because
it keeps you locked to where you are.

Life isn't about waiting for the storm to pass; it is about learning to dance in the rain.
Life is to be lived. And to live is to be an active participant in your life.
Time to pick it up. Life is simply too short to let it pass you by.
Time to get active!
The dance awaits.

You Are Where You Are

... because you have put yourself there.

Nothing ever happens to you in life.
You are co-creating each and every experience.

All experiences in life are important, especially the "painful" experiences
which always bring you to a much better place, unless of course
you allow yourself to go some other place with it.
Those painful experiences are what help you to bottom out and
clear the slate for a much better experience moving forward.
But sometimes we're not ready to move forward and we choose
(consciously or subconsciously) to stay in the painful space because
identifying with the pain somehow seems oddly comfortable.

When you cannot let go of a painful situation, be it love related,
work-related or friendship-related, then you are *CHOOSING*
to stay stuck in a situation that is no longer feeding you.
At that point you are being held responsible for where you are in life.
You own it. No one is keeping you back. You are the only one in your own way.
No one has control over your life unless you give it.
If you are unhappy with where you are,
you need to recognize that no one has put you in that box but yourself.
"Bad" things happen to "good" people all the time.
*But good people know how to move past the experience so they can move forward in
their lives.* They don't stay mired in the muck.
Keeping yourself stuck will assure you that
you will destroy your own life.

You are where you are because you have allowed yourself to be there.
If you don't like where you are, time to get out and move forward with your life.
Even if that change seems foreign and frightening,
I assure you nothing could be more frightening that staying in a dead
space where growth will never happen. It is true;
you are where you are because of your choices thus far.
But where you are headed is always supremely up to you.
Are you ready to own your own life?

Crossing Bridges

... will always take you to the other side.

Whatever that side may be.

Bridges are metaphors for the transitions in our lives.

Bridges take us from one place to another and
they usually bridge our past with our future.

But because they are not our past and they are not yet our future,
they represent that unknown in-between stage that can make many
people uneasy. We don't like uncertainty.

We like knowing where we will be at every step.

Life isn't like that.

Life requires you get on that transitional bridge and walk away from your past
(old job, old lover, etc.) and set out on a journey towards the future.

Sometimes the bridges are long ahead of you and
you cannot see your destination.

That does NOT mean that is isn't there.

Sometimes you have to walk in the dark and it might be hard
to find your way, *but there is always a handrail to guide you.*

On a bridge you do not have to think about where you are going.
You just have to keep going. *The path is set for you.*

You will get to where you need to be when it is time.

Just like on a bridge, your path in life is set for you.

The bridge you are on has to take you to your destination (your future).

It can be no other way. Trust the many bridges in your life.

These transitional spaces are meant for you to grow and enjoy the scenery

while on your walk towards the future.

You do not have to have all the answers in life.

You just have to keep walking.

As long as you are on your bridge,

you are guaranteed to get off at your destination.

So how do you know if you are on your bridge?

Staying stuck in the past will guarantee that

you never get to that bridge and trying to rush ahead and

take that speed boat across those waters

will jeopardize your journey. SLOW DOWN. Take a walk.

Even though you may not know where you are going,

if you keep walking, you will learn so much about yourself in the process and

you will be delivered precisely to the exact place, at the exact time

you needed to be there. Life is your journey;

keep moving forward and cross that bridge into the rest of your life.

If It Doesn't Challenge You

... it doesn't change you.

Challenges make you stronger.

Life is hard. It just is. It was never meant to be easy.

We do not learn by living an easy life.
We only learn by living through challenging experiences.
Those challenging experiences make you a better person.
If you can rise to the challenge and transform the pain or fear,
it brings you to a far better place.

We have all heard that challenges make you stronger, but how, exactly?
They make you wiser, more alert, more strategic, more willing
to take risks, more self-assured, more patient, more confident in
your own abilities, more optimistic, more empowered (less of a victim)
and more mindful in your approach to life.

You are NEVER a victim. Challenges don't happen to you to punish you
or keep you back in life. They happen to test your resolve and see how
strong and conscious you have become on your path.
Every time you overcome a perceived challenge,
you earn another level of conscious evolution.
And on the flip side, every time you allow yourself to fall down and
feel sorry for yourself, you take a step back.

Life is always about moving forward and doing whatever you need to do
to keep moving forward. *Challenges are not roadblocks; t
hey are opportunities to test ourselves to see if we are still growing in the direction we
want to be moving or if we have decided to stop growing all together.*
Victims stop living. Masters create lifetimes of great richness and beauty.

The mind is the only difference between the two.
Take control of your life and change your perception the next time
you hit a challenge. Don't let a closed door be an obstacle.
Learn to find the key and open the door yourself so you can keep moving
forward and create the life you truly deserve.

Life Doesn't Get Better By Chance

... it gets better by change.

Life changes. *Nothing stays the same.*
Nothing is ever MEANT to stay the same.
As humans, we are meant to grow and evolve and
that doesn't happen by staying still.
Movement initiates change.

But sometimes the idea of change seems overwhelming,
so we don't allow it. We would rather accept the dysfunction
that is familiar to us then to offer ourselves up for the unfamiliar.
Hence we get in the way of ourselves and our growth.

Do you want your life to change? Learn to get out of the way of yourself.
Stop trying to control the outcome. Life is meant to change naturally.
If it is not changing for you, you might be holding onto something/
someone/some thought that is keeping you back from moving forward.

Do you want freedom? Do you want change?
Do you want to feel as if you are living the best life you can?
Get out of the way of yourself. Allow life to change for you.
Don't hold onto things and people that you think are the answers.
They may not be.

As soon as you learn to let go and let life be,
you will take more chances, undertake more risks and
initiate newer courses of action that are unfamiliar to you.
This movement is what brings about change.
Change never comes about through complacency and waiting.
No more waiting for your life to change, invite change in, step up to the plate and let go
of old habits and thought patterns that are clearly not serving you.
If things have not changed in awhile, it is time to do something new and
it is that movement that will usher in change.
Time to change; what are you waiting for?

When You Hit a Wall

... you have NO choice but to change direction.

Where else can you go?

Walls are put in place for a reason - to STOP you dead in your tracks, and they serve their purpose.

Think of life as a maze – you are going along smoothly and
all of a sudden you hit a wall. Fine. No drama.
You are stopped and you pick a new direction.
The wall was your indication that you can no longer
move in that direction.

It is the same thing in life – when you hit a wall,
it is your indication that you are being blocked from progressing further.
It is time for you to now make another decision to proceed along a new
direction and chart a new course. *No drama needed; only change is required.*

Hitting a wall is not a problem.
*Deciding to IGNORE the wall and NOT turn towards a new direction
is really the problem.* If the wall is there,
the universe is telling you to explore other options.
Of course, you can use your free will and climb over the wall,
but there may just be a better way to move forward in your life.
Why make things difficult? If you come up against a wall,
stop and yield to it. It might be trying to tell you something.
Turn towards a new direction and you may just find that
it brings you to a much better place.

Learn to Take One Step

... the universe will do the rest.

We don't become huge successes overnight. Nor do we find our passions,
our soul-mates or our life purposes over night.
The journey to become ourselves can take a lifetime.
But that lifetime begins with one step.

We often judge ourselves for where we are and
what we have accomplished. You do not need
the perfect solution for your problems, the perfect game plan for success
or the perfect strategy to find a mate, *all you need to do is take one step,*
any step in any direction will invite the powers of destiny to join you.

Once you open the door and open your energy to "the next step,"
the universe will support you on your path. You are never alone.
Taking one step releases energetic blockages that might otherwise be holding you back.
Taking that one step (especially when you do not know where it will lead
you) will bring opportunities and connections to you
that you would have never dreamed of.

The journey of a lifetime always begins with one step.
You do not need all the answer to take that one step.
You just have to take it. No more fear.
Your life begins the moment you can take that one step.
What are you waiting for?

Do You Want To Change The World?

... start by changing yourself.

It all starts with YOU.
As Gandhi said, "BE the change you want to see in the world."

We never realize our power.
We never realize just how much influence
we personally have in the world.
We never think we can make a difference by ourselves.
We are very wrong.

Every act of kindness, every smile, every compliment we give
changes our molecular structure.
It shifts our energy and helps us to create more light in the world.
Not only do you feel better, but the planet responds in kind.

When we focus on spreading love and kindness, our planet heals.
When we focus on spewing venom towards each other, competing with
each other and building our personal wealth to the detriment of being
kind to the person hurting next to us, we've lost the lesson.
Selfishness breeds pain and misery on a personal & global level.

Natural disasters are Mother Earth's response to hate, anger, misused
power, greed, materialism and waste. *Do you want to change the world?*
Start by changing yourself. Put more positive energy out into the universe in small ways
everyday. Smile at a stranger – compliment your colleague –
offer to help someone in need – small random acts of kindness
will go a long way to helping you live the best life you can.

Circumstances do not change outside of you until you undergo a change on the inside.
Embrace positive energy and share it with others.
You might just find that the things you are looking for in life
find their way miraculously to your door.

Be the change you want to see in the world.
And the world will change around you.
What are you waiting for?

Chapter 7

Emotional Well-being

You should always take responsibility
for your own emotional well-being.

In your dealings with others,
the best advice I can give you is to *know what is yours and
give the rest back.*

In other words, know what behaviors are yours and
what behaviors are NOT yours.
Never accept responsibility for others' bad behavior,
but at the same time, never put
your behaviors unconsciously on others.

By applying a degree of consciousness
to our lives and our relationships with others,
we can begin to understand our own emotionality
and not blame others for our own issues.

It's no one's job to fix you or save you from yourself.
It's your job.
Get crackin' on it.

Chapter 7

Emotional Well-being

How well do you know yourself? Do you accept responsibility for your own emotional well-being, or do you put it on others? Do you expect other people to fix or save you from yourself? Guess what? It's no one's job to sort you out; it's YOUR job.

I spend my life sorting people's emotional wellbeing and helping them to distinguish their issues from that of their partners', colleagues', families', etc. I plant new seeds with them and help them to understand where their work is and what their responsibility is in terms of healing certain emotional issues.

It's not easy. When you are dealing with people's emotions, lots of stuff comes up. Many people do not want to see what is right in front of them, so they bury it deep within themselves – so deep, in fact, that they have no idea that those issues are actually theirs. They just very sharply REACT to another person's behavior and then blame the other person for everything because it is easier than looking in the mirror at themselves. Deeply disturbed people engage in this type of behavior. What's worse is that they generally have no idea they are doing it. Somehow it's always someone else's issue, never theirs. Funny how that works. And just for the record, "deeply disturbed" is also nicely disguised as "highly functioning" – on the surface you would never know. But I generally do.

As a teacher and coach, I tend to sniff out the dysfunction in someone quickly. Call it an occupational hazard if you will. For the most part, I can see what is going on with them and I feel as if it is my responsibility to call it out for them, bring it to their conscious awareness and help give them tools to heal it. But not everyone is ready to do that type of work on themselves.

I had a short-term involvement with someone in 2014 who is literally bigger than life – big personality, 6'5" sturdy build, large energy field, strong magnetism, deep, loud penetrating voice. When he walks into a room, you know it. But he is not subtle when he approaches people; he can be very overwhelming. That big personality serves him in his media career, but limits him in his personal interactions because he lacks sensitivity to people's boundaries, people's needs and people's comfort zones (although he is one of the most sensitive creatures you will ever meet). There's no other word for it – this person is INTENSE and highly unconscious of his behavior. He has been told before by many people that he is intense. Intensity is NOT a connective type of personality; it actually does the opposite. It assures that you will NOT connect with someone because it makes people uncomfortable and pushes people away.

Now, I should remind you that I am clairsentient, so I not only listen to what is being said to me, I can also feel what is more prominent underneath the surface. When I first met him, I could tell how beautiful and sensitive his heart was and how sincere his intention was to put good out into the world and to be a good person. But, of course, I could also see many of his connection issues upfront. I saw them that first evening. Within that first hour of meeting him, he told me both everything and nothing at all. I knew he wanted marriage, kids, talked about moving to California with me, etc. - everything that would send someone running on a first date! He also told me that he was engaged once before, but it fell through. When I asked why it fell through, I was told, "Well, for every reason — we differed in our financial views, political, social, family, etc…" There was no deeper explanation and it was never brought up again over the next nine months.

People who are not looking to really connect with you will say everything up front with the subconscious intention of setting a boundary and pushing you away. Then they go silent. There is nothing more to say, nothing more to share. They've put it out there and now they're done. They might tell themselves they are seeking a relationship, but under the surface, they are screaming inside and saying everything that will scare you away from being deeply involved with them. His intensity actually protects himself from creating real, deep connections with others. It's a subconscious defense mechanism, and one which he has perfected.

I knew it. I saw it. I called it, but I stayed in it to help this person learn about himself, because I really saw the beauty in his heart and in his wanting to be loved. So, in essence, I learned first-hand what it was to be involved with someone who's *emotionally unavailable* and/or considered to be *emotionally immature*. Unfortunately, this is very common, especially amongst men (although it certainly doesn't exclude women), and especially amongst men who are 40+ years and never married — it's true, there really IS a reason why they are not!

The tough thing about emotionally unavailable individuals is that they do NOT see themselves as such and will continue to date - sending MIXED SIGNALS that they actually want to be in a committed relationship. In my case, this particular man is very sensitive and romantic and is also incredibly affectionate. He speaks with terms of endearment and whispers sweet nothings - but yet, nothing goes deeper

Chapter 7

Emotional Well-being

than that. He was unable to share his feelings/express his emotions. He was like a wall – too busy protecting himself, his emotions and his interests to let anyone penetrate it.

I soon realized that there was nothing below the surface when he could only have phone conversations that were less than seven minutes, couldn't read emails at all and could only process text messages that were no more than two lines. Anything you would want to share about yourself at any given moment was too much information for him. He would shut down by changing the subject and ending the conversation quickly before the topic would go deep - "I gotta go, baby," and the line goes silent.

He also exhibits another tell tale sign of emotional unavailability - his relationships only last three months, and the women usually leave him. He sets it up that way. He still has not seen this pattern and he has been running it for at least 20 years.

Now, the real irony is that this being seeks connection; he desperately wants to be connected to others, he really does, so he connects very superficially with EVERYONE. Because he wants connection, he wants to be friends with everyone and he gets it through lots of superficial, trite connections where no one really needs anything from him (especially lovers). But, they like him, see him as a "good guy" and therefore they are there for him if he needs to call on them (usually for a work-related favor). This is the type of connection that works best for him because it keeps him and his interests safe and protected from hurt. It might be helpful to know that his father left his family when he was four and he has spent the rest of his life guarding his heart and building up defenses against real, deep connections that could lead to love. Deeply loving in his book translates to a "fear of losing that love when it walks out the door." It breaks my heart every time I think about him; I just want to hug his pain away.

Why did I share all that? Not because I am upset with this beautiful man. I adore him and always have, but I want you to understand the importance of emotional well-being. This beautiful man lives on the façade of his own life, never letting himself go deeper. The emotional walls he has built up for himself at this point in his life will take a lifetime to tear down if he is lucky. But unfortunately for him, there is no conscious awareness of this behavior. And without it, change can never happen.

When we can see our issues and have the awareness to catch the patterns upfront, then the patterns no longer have any control over us, and we are truly free. My fear for this man is that he will continue on this path of trying to superficially connect

Chapter 7

Emotional Well-being

with many others, but miss the opportunity to allow himself to be in a REAL truly loving relationship. But you cannot fix people, and you cannot save them, and that is my lesson here.

In my life, I am a natural mirror for people. Trust me, they don't always like what they see when they look at me (or hear what I have to say). They are really seeing themselves play out, and then they have a tendency to lash out at me and blame me for it. What I had done wrong in that specific relationship was that I stayed in it too long trying to help him see what I could see. However, he was not ready to do that work, and so the fact that I was highlighting the issue(s) made me the bad guy and the one who was being "hyper-critical of him." I am not a critical person at all, but if I see unconscious or unkind behavior, I feel the need to remedy it. I was becoming progressively frustrated with his inability to see his own behavior, and he wouldn't give me the audience time to be able to articulate it. If I would bring up anything that wasn't positive, I was slammed and told that he didn't want to be "criticized and wasn't looking for unsolicited advice." On my path, I am learning that you cannot help people who do not want your help.

It is getting better for me though. I have been breaking that pattern in recent relationships, but I highlight it for you to see that we all have patterns in relationships. It is really important that you learn to own what's yours and give the rest back, otherwise, you will only succeed in taking on other people's stuff. And why would you want to carry other people's baggage? We have enough ourselves to carry, don't we?

The following essays are my words of advice on how to recognize what behaviors might be yours and what might NOT be yours. Learn to recognize the difference, and I promise you, it will transform your relationships.

When You Get Angry

... it's never about someone else.

It's ALWAYS about YOU.

Just like happiness is not contingent on anything outside of you,
it comes from within. So does anger,
but we rarely understand this concept.
We like to pretend that it's everyone else's fault that
they somehow "made us angry."
Truth is, they were just
triggers to bring out the anger that we already have inside of us.

Blaming others for our apparent anger issues is deconstructive.
It is never anyone else's fault that you cannot control
your emotional state. You have a choice every day as to whether or not
you will ALLOW someone to push your buttons and make you angry.
If you engage that very impulse, you have chosen to give your power over
to another human being to make you angry.
It is always a choice — *a choice to react to that other person as if their dysfunction
was yours or it is a choice to be FREE of them and their dysfunction.*
That choice is always yours.

Recognize that you do not have to dance with someone's crazy.
If crazy makes you angry, learn to disengage from their dance.
You can still spend time with that person; you just do not need
to make yourself responsible for pointing out their bad behavior.
If you don't claim it as your own, it shouldn't have any effect over you.

Finally, *don't stay angry with people who anger you.*
Those people are only there to show you
your own tendency towards anger.
Thank them for raising the emotion in you
so that now you may heal it.
They are doing you a great service if you learn from your behavior.
If you don't, you will just stay angry.

When Crazy Comes Knocking

... send it packing

You cannot negotiate with crazy.
Nothing rings more true in life.
We all innately understand this yet we all find ourselves
from time to time trying to negotiate with crazy.

Here's the bottom line...
negotiating with crazy (in any way, shape or form) makes you just as crazy.
It really does. In life, it is important to get your point across and express
yourself, but at the instant you realize that you are not getting
through to another person, *walk away.*
Yours is not to convince someone of your being right.
Yours is to know yourself, know that you have done the best job you can
do whether it be working, communicating, responding to another, etc...
Once you know you have done all you can do, put the gun down,
put your hands up and walk away – WALK AWAY.

The time you spend arguing and trying to convince others of
your righteousness, deprives you of the opportunity to move ahead
in your life and what you gain instead is a period of misery, negativity,
frustration, anger and confusion. Why do this to yourself?
If people do not understand you and you have made yourself
quite clear to them, then you have no regrets.
Remember that some people will always be incapable of hearing you.
And unfortunately that is not something you will ever be able to change.
Everyone has their own issue that may prevent them from hearing
what it is you are saying.

When you buy into crazy's way of thinking, you own it.
You make it your own and you take yourself down with
the fight to make yourself clear.
It is not crazy that destroys us;
it is in the dance with crazy that we lose ourselves and our power.
When crazy comes knocking, definitely smile and send it packing!
You will be better for it.

Envying Others

... makes sure you never get what they have.

People are only jealous and envious of others
when they themselves are not living up to their OWN potential.

Instead of being inspired and driven to achieve what others have,
there is a tendency to become resentful that
we do not yet have it in our hands at that moment.
The result is that we generate a high degree of
low vibrational energy (resentment, jealousy and envy)
which creates a wall and separates us from ever achieving it.
That wall of negativity puts you on lock down so you are unable to
attract anything positive into your life.
It keeps you from your own happiness.

Envy and jealousy are cop outs. You can have whatever you want in life.
Everything is available to you if you open up to source and
allow it to come to you.
Nobody gets anything that you cannot have. It's up to you to set out to get it.

You are not being punished. Nothing is being withheld from you.
If you desire it in your life, get up and do something about it.
*Make change in your life so you can bring about the opportunities or
the materiality that you so desire.*

Life is about choices – every day.
Where you put your energy determines your next experience.
Are you going to give your energy over to other people whom you are
jealous/envious of OR are you going to allow yourself to use them
as inspiration to bring about everything that your heart desires?

The choice is always yours.
Blowing out other people's candles will NEVER make yours burn brighter.
Wish them well and allow them to inspire you
to make the change necessary to make your own dreams come true.
Life is too short to sit on the sidelines and jealously mock the winning team;
get out there and make sure you score your own goals.

When You Are Alone

... you can see where you are.

When you are with others, you have NO idea.

Being alone at any stage in your life represents an enforced separation.
It is the universe's way of giving you space to reflect and
help you work out something that you would otherwise not see.

In life we tend to busy ourselves from
looking in the mirror and doing our work.
When lovers, friends and/or jobs get taken away from you,
it is a sign that a part of your life needs attention.
Once your plate is cleared and there is some space,
you can begin to see what needs to be healed.

Being alone is one of the greatest gifts the universe can bestow upon us.
It gives us the space to process our life path and
gives us the clarity we need to make changes that will help us to move
forward in the right direction.
Don't rush to "busy yourself" when you find yourself alone.
You will miss the opportunity to heal the part of yourself
that has been screaming for attention.
When you are with others, those parts of ourselves get buried
in favor of prioritizing others' needs or others' behaviors.

Enjoy your alone time and give gratitude
for the opportunity to allow yourself to heal.
It is in that space of being alone that great change comes about.
And it is only through being alone that you can see where you really are in life.
Embrace your alone time and use it as
the stepping stone to take stock of the rest of your life.
Oddly enough, spending time alone is really
the only way to find true happiness with all others.

People Who Criticize

... are usually the ones who have the most work to do.

Everyone has issues. EVERYONE.

Conscious people are the ones who KNOW
what their issues are and do not blame others
for their own shortcomings.
But not everyone is conscious.
Not everyone owns up to their inadequacies.

One of the major life lessons a person can have
is known as "self-perfection".
Individuals with this life lesson are here
to do serious work on themselves – to "perfect themselves,"
so to say. But all too often, those with this life lesson
may become somewhat misguided,
and as a result demand perfection of everyone around them
instead of themselves.
It is easier for them to find fault
in you than it is for them to turn the mirror on themselves.

Those who continually find fault in others are generally those who have
the most work to do on themselves and they are conveniently avoiding
looking at their own behavior.

Do your work.

Know what your issues are and give the rest back.

Don't own what is not yours.

If you take it on, you will start to embody it in no time.

When your critics start to judge you,

you should be able to detach from their commentary with a sense of ease.

Recognize that the person you are dealing with

is having issues doing their own work.

Yours is not to save them or fix them.

Yours is to not own their criticisms.

Yours is to turn the mirror back on them and walk away with your head up high.

Owning "what is yours" empowers you;

it holds you responsible and accountable for your life.

It makes you stronger and wiser and

brings great rewards to the table for you.

Those who prefer holding others accountable are not

accepting responsibility for their life.

They are the ones who remain lost –

for without blame they have no sense of recourse.

For sure, they remain stuck by their own hand.

Take control back of your life.

Own what is yours and turn the mirror back on those who just cannot see.

Fear Clips Your Wings

... but you were always meant to soar.

Fear is a powerful emotion that comes on
to protect you from a perceived harm.
Fear keeps you "safely" out of situations and keeps you in your nest.
But you do not grow in your nest.
You only grow from learning what it feels like to fall out of your nest and
learn to take flight on your own.
You expand your horizons and go to new places and create new nests —
this is the game of life.

It is important to keep tabs on fear or it has the ability to take over our lives.
Often times, fear manifests as anxiety and panic attacks.
When you feel anxiety and panic, it's the body's way of trying to protect
you from a situation or a person you deem harmful.

Fear is also your indicator that you are dealing with a life lesson.
Anxiety and panic are nothing more than a trigger for you
to realize that the discomfort you are feeling is because you are dancing
face to face with one of your life lessons —
and that is NEVER easy. Here is where the work begins.

Fear would have you run from your life lesson and never learn it –
maybe take a pill to quiet the trigger and
numb the reminder that you have work to do.
You can only do that for so long,
your lessons always come back with a vengeance.
The work is in recognizing where your patterns are and shedding light on them.
Once you realize where the anxiety is coming from,
you can begin to heal the experience and
apply wisdom to help you move forward in your life.

The answer is always to move through the fear so you can transform it.
If you find yourself avoiding situations so
to not experience the discomfort of fear,
then you are hiding in your nest.
You can spend a lifetime in your nest. Ask yourself if you really want to do that.
When there is a whole world out there for you to see and
you have a beautiful set of wings, it might be time to spread them and take flight.
Taking flight is the only thing that will transform your fear.

Time to leap out of that nest. If you allow yourself to stay there,
fear will certainly clip your wings and you will never learn to fly.
What options do you really have?

When People Are Never Happy With You

... they are unhappy with themselves.

We always want to be accepted and respected and sometimes
we come up against people who it seems are never happy with anyone or
anything. You know the type – the boss who you can never please; the
partner who always wants you to be better; the friend
who is always competing with you. Where does this come from?

It comes from an overall lack of contentedness in oneself.
After all, how can you be happy with anyone if
you are not happy with yourself first? This is where it begins.

If someone is feeling great about themselves, they are usually on
top of the world and that helps them to relate better to other people.
But when someone is feeling down and maybe unhappy with their weight,
feeling not good enough at their job and with their performance in a
relationship, then they find it extremely difficult to connect with others
and see the beauty in others. But whose fault is that?

We tend to take on others' unhappiness with themselves and make it about us.
In those instances, *it is NEVER about you.*
Remember you cannot control others and their opinions of you or themselves.
That is not the name of the game. The name of the game is
to *be happy with yourself* and feel good enough in your skin
so that other people's comments and opinions simply roll off you.
They should never stick to you unless you want them to.

The next time you are feeling that someone is not treating you kindly and
isn't happy with you, send them love and realize that it is not you that
they are unhappy with, it is themselves.
For if they were truly happy with themselves, *they would be able to communicate
with you in a much more fair, kind and motivating fashion.*
If they are being unkind, unfair or mean, it is most likely about them.
Never make others' unhappiness with themselves about you.
It is your happiness with yourself that is the key to setting you free.
Are you happy with yourself?

Complicated People

... make everything complicated.

The energy you put out into the world is the exact energy you get back.
So why not try and make things easier on yourself?

Complicated people make things difficult for themselves
because of the way they show up in life.
When you learn how to relax into stressful situations,
you moderate the outcomes.
Things get easier when you choose the simpler path.
Most of us do not know how to do this because we think more is better.
More is never better, it is just more.
And if anything, it makes things more complicated and
sets an energetic pattern of resistance into play for you.

Here's a tip: *there is no need to over-think situations and*
no need to over-plan situations.
The most successful solutions are ALWAYS the SIMPLEST.

Remember, complicated people create complicated relationships and
complicated situations. Their lives become complicated by their own hand.
Recognize that you are in control and
if you want things to be less stressful and more relaxed,
learn to streamline.

Simplifying calms and soothes your experience.
Complications create disharmony and chaos.

Your life is up to you.
You have a choice every day as to how you are going to show up.
Are you going to stress yourself out by trying to do everything at once or
are you going to pare back and take the path that optimizes
your resources and time?
Learn to streamline your life and everything will be less complicated.

The Emotional Roller Coaster

... we have all jumped on board and gone for the ride.

How enjoyable is it really?
For those of us who are emotionally balanced, it is NOT.
For those of us learning the very difficult life lesson of "finding balance" in life,
it proves to be an on-going ride of extremes.

This is how it works....
those who seek to be balanced will be continually drawn into high drama
situations with high drama people and lots of crisis and chaos along the way.
In other words, *they undergo a type of life plan that continually sends them into
high-highs and low-lows over and over again.*
This wild swing is meant to make them so miserable that
they learn to STOP reaching for what they think is
going to make them feel better
(a drink, drug, food, unhealthy relationship, travel escape, etc.) and
begin to start slowing down the rate of the swing
to find themselves at their own center point.

The important thing to remember in life is that no one intentionally
chooses to torture themselves, per se.
They choose to undergo this difficult learning lesson so that they can
grow and evolve into a healthier and happier being –
one who fully understands that his/her happiness will not be found
in an impulsive reach for extremes.

By experiencing ourselves out of balance time and time again,
we can begin to start finding our own center point.

It doesn't end here…
once you have found your own center point and
achieved supreme balance in yourself, it is critical that
you NOT impulsively jump on someone else's emotional roller coaster ride!
In other words, once you have learned this lesson yourself and
you consciously decide to join forces with another
who has NOT yet learned this lesson,
know that doing so will be intensifying your own experience –
you will now be on THEIR emotional roller coaster of life.

If you have already learned this lesson,
it is important to find someone who possesses the same amount of stability,
security and emotional peace you have already found in yourself.
If you want life to be easier, calmer and more centered,
learn to slow down your swing and for sure,
learn to stay off other people's swing sets.

What You Focus On Expands

... so focus on what you want, not what you don't.

Everything is energy and where we put our focus is what we will continue
to experience – whether we want to experience it or not.

It's very simple.
You do not get what you want in life by focusing on what you do NOT want.

In life, we only attract a vibrational experience that
matches our own vibration.
So, if our feeling is sadness and frustration and our focus is on
that which we do not like about our significant other or job,
then we will only succeed in creating more of the same because
that is where our focus is.
Whereas if we were to focus on the positive aspects of our relationship
and/or job, then we would be raising our vibration and
therefore able to attract a much higher outcome.

You have to feel good to have good in your life.
If you feel badly, you will only be able to attract those situations
that are unpleasant and unsatisfactory.
If you do not feel as if there is any good in your life to focus on,
then focus on your dreams.
When you focus on that which you truly want,
and that which will truly make you happy,
then that is all you need to feel good and then the universe can respond
accordingly by bringing you more of that good feeling.
This is the law of attraction –
it is a spiritual law of the universe and cannot be changed.

When we learn how the universe works, we learn how to get what we want out of life.
If you continually feel badly and focus on what you do not have,
you will only create more lack and unhappiness.
Time to learn how to play the game. Focusing on what you do not want
in your life can never bring you that which you truly desire, so focus on
what you do want. It's the only way to make sure you get it.

Overcoming Obstacles

Obstacles and hardship are part of the human experience.
They are not meant to limit you or stop you;
they are meant to make you GREAT.

The challenging times in our lives are the most rewarding
times because they are the times
when we do the most growth.

*It doesn't matter what happens to you in life, it only matters
that you make your life better because of it.*

When you can learn to reframe all experiences in your life
to become challenges not obstacles,
you begin to find your position of strength.
You also begin to realize that you are in control of your life
and that your life is NEVER in control of you.

You are NEVER a victim of your life; you are a master of it.

All obstacles/challenges are only in place to make you better,
and when *you can learn*
to get the lesson and get out,
you move forward in your life at breakneck speed.

Chapter 8

Overcoming Obstacles

By far I would say that this is the most significant chapter in my book. It all comes down to how we reframe the challenging situations in our lives. Do we sit back and allow ourselves to play the victim or do we apply a degree of mastery over the situation and learn to find the lesson and get out so we can move forward with our lives?

Trust me, I wrote the book on overcoming obstacles. Nothing in my life was handed to me. I did have somewhat of a privileged upbringing but that was balanced with extreme emotional turmoil from a young age. I come from a close family (Italian descent), am the oldest of four and the only girl. When I was 15, my seven-year-old brother woke up crying with a 107 fever one morning. Now, if you knew Michael, he was a spirited, mischievous, but frail little boy who always seemed to be getting sick and/or complained about stomach aches and everything under the sun. I never used to give his whining much attention, but on this morning, my intuition felt a sense of complete empathy for him and deep sadness that I never understood. He was sobbing in his bed and kept saying that his leg hurt over and over. He called to me as I was getting ready to leave for the bus stop. He said, "Donna can you help me, please? My leg really hurts. It really hurts." I told him he would be fine and to go back to bed and I would see him after school. I knew my parents were still home, so he was in good hands if he needed help. But needless to say, *I never saw him again*. He died 24 hours later of spinal meningitis. The pain in his leg was in fact bruising due to hemorrhaging. It was a folly of errors with doctor's offices and hospitals, but by the time they had the results of his spinal tap, he was gone.

That event forever changed me. His death set me on a lifelong journey of wanting to understand the spirit world. His death has made me who I am today. It would have been easy to fall apart and blame God or the Divine for taking my brother but instead, I used that as a platform for understanding how things work in life and what we are all doing here. I have taken that very difficult emotional experience and transformed it into a position of strength. It has allowed me to find the strength in myself to keep going throughout life's difficult experiences and has given me the tools to continue to inspire clients and students to do the same.

That experience along with many other emotional challenges in my life has directed me along my path towards helping others and inspiring them to live their best lives. There is a great saying, "we are not measured by our joyous achievements,

Chapter 8

Overcoming Obstacles

but by who we are in our darkest moments. It is here that we find ourselves." It is through my darkest emotional pain that I have managed to learn to pick myself up, dust myself off, put the pieces back together the best way I know how in that moment and keep walking with my head up high. By doing so each and every time, I have managed to make my life circumstances better. I have found that each time I pick myself up and wipe away the tears, the sun comes out again and rewards me generously.

Life is not going to be without its challenges/obstacles. The question remains: "How will you handle them when they show up?" We always have a choice, and personally I will always choose to make myself better because of having had those experiences. They will never take me down. My life is too precious to give my power over to anyone or any situation to make me feel like a victim. I am a master of my life, and because I see things that way, I continue to grow and evolve and reap the benefits of a life well lived. You can do the same.

Below are my essays to help inspire you in your darkest moments. I hope they give you the encouragement and understanding of how to deal with life's difficulties as they come up. They will give you the strength and tools necessary to help you reframe those obstacles and redefine better circumstances for yourself. After all, perception is reality, and when you can learn to change your perception of what is going on in your life, you will change your reality of it. It can be no other way.

... your work is to make your life BETTER *because of it.*

End of story.

In life you always have a choice.
A choice to either fall into the victimhood of the "bad" situation or
you can muster up the energy to pick yourself up and
transform the "bad" into something even better.

The choice to either let the situation destroy you or strengthen you is always yours.
How you look at a situation determines its power over you.
And how you respond to a situation determines
the quality of your next life experience.

All bad experiences only happen to bring you to a better and higher place.
The difficult situations are the real gifts – that's where the real learning/
growing takes place. The happier situations are just the rewards;
there is no real growth during those periods.

When you can learn to pick yourself up after every fall,
dust yourself off and keep going – the best way you know how –
the universe always responds in kind and the rewards are tenfold.
When you work towards your highest outcome, the universe will work
with you to help you achieve that outcome.
But when you slump into the lower outcome,
it will let you sit there alone in your misery.

Do you want to rise up and live your best life? Keep searching for the higher place.
Reframe all situations so that your life can be on the up-and-up.
You will be given every assistance along the way as long as
you are walking the higher side of your path.

When bad things happen,
it is your job to make things better for yourself – any way possible.
When you can get into the habit of becoming better for having had those
experiences, the universe will bring you everything you desire.
The choice is always yours.

Speed Bumps Slow You Down

... so you can proceed with caution.

Not everything in our lives is meant to happen instantaneously.
Some situations take time to cultivate.
But in our society we are so trained in *instant gratification* so that when
things don't go according to our plan, we get frustrated and anxious and
impatient and try to force situations to come about unnaturally.

*It is important to note that on our planet everything works on its own timeline and
NOTHING can be rushed.*
The universe maintains perfect time management in terms of bringing
you the situations you need, exactly when you need them.
There is no room for negotiation here. As we know,
things happen for a reason and they happen quite when they are supposed to.

So, why is it that we encounter speed bumps in our lives?
Why doesn't everything happen when we want it to?
The answer is easy. When you hit a speed bump,
it is an *enforced period of reflection & analyses*
where you are being asked to proceed forward with caution.
In essence, *you are being held back from what you think you want/ need and are
being asked to evaluate the situation and your role within it.*
Are you sure you are ready to go there?
Do you have all the tools you need in place to manage that next step?
Is this opportunity truly going to meet your needs?
Have you considered other possibilities?
These are all reasons why we hit speed bumps – it is a *built-in process to
protect us from jumping into situations that might NOT be right for us.*

The road ahead is always uncertain, but you can be certain that when you
hit a speed bump, you are being asked to slow down and
process the direction you are heading.
If the path ahead was clear for you, you wouldn't hit a speed bump.
Heed the warning and use the time to evaluate what's ahead of you.
You might decide you don't even want to be on that road.
Speed bumps are the disruptions that bring ultimate clarity.

Forcing Things To Happen

... doesn't make them happen for you.

Learning to relax into your life does.

We always think we have all the answers, but in reality, we seldom do.
Learn to see the patterns.
*Learn to see when something is not working for you and
be able to walk away from it.*

Life is a balance between grace and effort.
You need to put forth the effort to achieve anything in life,
but you also need to be able to abandon efforts
when the results continually prove undesirable.
*Learning to let go of the outcome with a sense of ease and grace
is one of our greatest tools to achieving the life of our dreams.*

Pushing and pushing doesn't make you stronger;
it weakens the very fabric you are trying to uphold.
The answer is NEVER in forcing things to be a certain way;
*the answer is in learning to accept that there may be a different way
that you have not thought about.*

True strength is not found in force, but in the ability to step back and allow.
Learning to allow life to happen instead of just forcing your agenda on it
will ensure that you receive the best outcome for your highest good.

*Don't force an issue. If it isn't working for you, back off and look at it from another
perspective.* Are you more interested in being right or doing the right thing?
If your ego cannot help you find your way,
the ability to step back and change perspective will.

You can use your free will to force an outcome for yourself,
or you can step back and allow fate to bring you to exactly
where you need to be. Which one do you think will make you most happy?
Remember, we don't always know what is right for us.
Stepping back can assure us of the opportunity to get a clear perspective.
Stop forcing things to happen and start enjoying the journey of your life.
You might be pleasantly surprised.

If It Is Showing Up In Your Life

... it's there to teach you something.

Otherwise it wouldn't be happening.

Nothing ever shows up around us
that doesn't somehow reflect what's going on inside of us.
Believe it or not, all events that occur in our lives
are our barometers for what we need to work on.

People mistakenly think that they are disconnected from the drama and
complications in their lives. They feel that somehow
these events are just happening to them and that
they are innocent bystanders.
*Nothing ever shows up in your life
that doesn't have a reason for being. Nothing.*

Events happen in our lives for many reasons, some of which to:
- bring to light an issue that needs to be worked through
- change direction on your path and open you up to something new
- make you stronger and give you the tools to strengthen your coping mechanisms
*- slow you down/stop you in your tracks and get you to focus on what is right in front
of you instead of what you are chasing*

Needless to say, if it is showing up in your life,
it is on YOUR path and it is meant for YOU to experience.
So make the most of the experience and realize
that you are not a victim of the events in your life,
you are the master of the program.
Start applying consciousness to your life.

Ask yourself why these events might be happening?
What are you meant to get out of them?
What do you need to learn or change or grow from?
Consciousness helps you to take responsibility for your life.
Once you take responsibility and own your life,
the rest is simply a walk in the park.

The Art Of The Fall

... is in learning to catch yourself.

We are all going to fall. It is written into the very fabric of our lives.
*But how we experience that fall determines the quality of our life
and our future experiences.*

If we could understand that the "fall" is just a vehicle for our growth
as it brings opportunity for us to learn critical lessons,
then we would be able to escape from the overall drama of the experience itself.
Remember our work is to GET THE LESSON and GET OUT
so that progress may be made and
our lives can move forward more constructively.

Experiencing the art of the fall is in learning to land more gracefully –
NOT going down in flames screaming obscenities to our imagined foes.
*When you start to recognize that your challenges are what determine
your potential for greatness, then there is no need to fight them.*

We live in a world of illusion. The great yogis call this "maya."
Life is an illusion. *There is no challenge greater than you in life and
there is no challenge that is out to get you and destroy you.*
The illusion would have you believe that you are unsafe and
"coming apart from the seams."
This illusion is just the vehicle to test what you have learned thus far to
see how you have grown or if you've grown at all.

Don't buy into the drama. It doesn't matter WHAT happens to you or
WHO does it.
*It only matters what you do with the outcome and how you make your life better
because of it.*
You can't control the fall, but you can absolutely control its effect over you.

The next time you face a major challenge in your life, remember that it is
never about the actual fall itself;
the wisdom is found in learning the reasons WHY you are falling.
Once you learn those lessons, you will never fall quite the same way again.

When Things Fall Apart

... it's time to put them together in a new way.

Nothing ever lasts forever. NOTHING.
*Things only fall apart when it is time to create something new and
something much better suited for you.*
You can only hold onto what is not working for you for so long before
the universe will take it away from you so that you can re-create
a much better situation for yourself.

Sometimes we cannot see and understand
what that better vision is for ourselves.
We get trapped in believing that if something falls apart on us that
we are somehow being punished and that we are victims trapped in the drama.
Instead of making positive change, we end up dwelling in the sadness of
the loss and the pain and confusion of the drama.
Sometimes we stay there for a very long time mourning the past,
but that is NOT where you are supposed to be.

The real work is in the understanding that you are never a victim of your life.
You are always the master and when you can see and understand that
*things only fall apart to help you create a better vision for yourself, you will begin to
understand how the universe works with you to help you to manifest your dreams.*

You always have a choice. You can either sit on the ground and feel sorry
for yourself for losing what was not working for you, OR
you can get busy excitedly putting together a new plan for yourself
that will better fit your needs.

When you learn the simple laws of the universe,
you begin to better understand your life.
You begin to learn that *when something falls apart,
it is an indication that it WAS NOT WORKING ANYMORE
and now you have a chance to find something that will work.*
When things fall apart, your work is to make your life better because of it.
There really is no other choice involved.
Get excited the next time your life falls apart.

Being Where You Don't Want To Be

... brings you to where you do.

We can't all be exactly where we want to be when we want to be there.
Life is a process. Suffice to say that
the way to get to where you want in life is
to live exactly where you are in the moment.
One step in front of the other brings you to your destination.
It can be no other way.

But in life, we seek instant gratification.
We prefer to skip steps in the process of our lives because we feel that
the destination is more important.
The destination is never more important
than is the journey to self-awareness.

Being where you don't want to be in life is a critical part of the process
of getting to where you DO want to be.
Learning the lesson in that moment is the key to unlocking the next phase of your life.
If you spend your time crying and lamenting where you are,
you haven't learned those lessons.
If you empower yourself to keep walking and learn from where you are,
the doors to your future open almost instantaneously.

You can get to wherever you want in life from right where you are.
In fact, it is spiritual law. There is no other way of getting there.
It is all about doing the work.
Recognize that you are where you are in your life for a reason and
when you learn certain lessons, you will be free to move onto the next phase.
There is NO punishment, there is NO being kept back and
there is NO reward being withheld from you.
Your ability to move forward in your life is directly contingent on your ability to be
where you are and fully experience and internalize the lessons of that moment
with ease, grace and gratitude.
There is no rush; you will get it when you truly get it.

Life Has No Remote

... you have to change the channel yourself.

Nothing good ever comes easily in life. Nothing.
If you want greatness, you have to work at it.
In our society we have become lazy at navigating our lives.

We prefer to sit back and press FAST FORWARD
through the uncomfortable bits to get to our goals.

We prefer to hit REWIND and sit stuck in past relationships and
situations that have long outlived their purpose in our lives.

But what we do not do enough of is to hit PLAY and
live in the moment and realize that as we are trying to fast forward our lives,
we are missing the spaces in between that could change us.
And when we are looking back at the REWIND,
we are not allowing ourselves to grow and evolve forward in the moment.

Living life in PLAY mode makes people uncomfortable
because they cannot control the outcome.
Life's outcomes are NEVER meant to be controlled.
They are meant to be lived through and experienced deeply.
You can only live your best life in PLAY mode.

Life has no remote.
If you allow it to play out,
you will be brought to the most optimal conclusion for your highest good.
If you try and use the remote,
you may just allow your free will to take you on a ride.

Time to throw out the remote. Be in the moment and allow your best life to play out.
Your transformation will happen while life is playing out before your very eyes.
Are you ready to play?

Focusing On Problems

... never brings solutions.

Simply put... *The less you think of trouble, the less of it you get.*
The more you think of things that please you, the better you will feel.
And the better you feel, the better things will go for you.

'Tis one of the spiritual laws of the universe.
But, in our society, we love to dwell on the negative, and
more importantly, we like to play the victim and wallow in states of self-pity.
Somehow we find solace in misery.
And as we know, misery loves company.

If we could remember that everything is energy and
everything that we attract to us is contingent on our energetic vibration,
then we would realize that we are supremely in control of our lives.
If we are filled with love and happiness and self-contentedness,
then every person and situation we attract to us will be loving,
supportive and happy. But if we are focused on self-loathing,
insecurity and fear, we will only succeed in drawing to us vibrational
matches to those low level energies.
And before you know it, we are surrounded with mean,
selfish and harsh people and situations.

Think: vibrational match. When you want to attract something,
you have to focus on those qualities – the perfect relationship,
the perfect job, happy friendships, etc., but at the same token,
if we do NOT WANT SOMETHING, we have to be very careful
NOT TO PUT OUR ATTENTION ON IT.
Our mere attention to the problem feeds the negative energy and
"stokes the fire." *If you do not want something in your life,*
DO NOT give it any attention. If you have to solve it, solve it quickly and
objectively and shut it down. Do not get entwined in the emotionality of
the situation. That negative emotionality is what will begin to bring forth
more of the same and only succeed in complicating your problems.
Not only do you get what you give, but you get what you think about.
If you do not want it in your life, do not give it any attention whatsoever.

You Can't Get To The Top

... if you're hangin' out on broken branches.

Life is like climbing a tree. Our path always takes us to the top.
With every lesson learned in a life, we move up,
closer to what it is we are searching for.
Our goal is to get to the top – in our own time,
of course – but to get to the top nonetheless.

The problem for most of us is that we get caught out on branches
that do NOT support us.
These branches may look supportive and even seem supportive at times,
but we may find ourselves on very shaky ground with them –
whether they be in the form of jobs, partners, friends, etc.

If you want to excel in life, you must be able to identify these broken branches and
move past them onto more stable limbs.
The real problems begin when we spend more time
trying to "fix" the broken branches and help them
to be more supportive of our needs. Why do that?
Why expend the energy to fix the very foundation that is not honoring you?
Wouldn't it be best to keep moving upward and rely on a stronger and
better foundation to do so?

We get caught up in the dramas of life and forget that our responsibility
is to ourselves and that we need to keep climbing to the top.
We get sidetracked and think that our responsibilities are to fix the broken
branches beneath our feet.
Those branches are broken for a reason.
They are teaching you where to step next time and what to watch out for.
Don't try and fix them; learn from them.
The goal is to make YOURSELF better, not the branches.

Life goes on whether you continue your journey up the tree or you
choose to spend your time saving branches. It's always your choice.
Choose the path that is going to bring you to where you want to be in life.

Breaking Bad

... is the only way to reveal the good.

Believe it or not, there is NO bad.
There is only our perception of bad that makes it real for us.

Any event we may perceive as "bad" in our lives only happens in order to bring us to a better place. All challenges and obstacles whether it be job loss,
loss of a loved one, bankruptcy, illness, etc. are purely illusions put in our
way so that we can learn how to be strong in ourselves and
strive to make our lives better because of it.
So bad is a catalyst for good — but only if you rise to the challenge and overcome it.
If you choose to buy into the bad, you can make it yours
for all of eternity and wear it as a jaded badge of honor.
But why would you do that?

Bad is only present until you do the work on transforming it.
Then bad becomes the highest version of good you could have ever
dreamed up for yourself. It is the way the universe works.
*It doesn't matter what has happened to you in your childhood or as an adult,
your work is to make your life better because of having had those experiences.*
When you make positive change for yourself,
not only does your life improve, but you inspire others to do the same.

When you consciously choose to break bad,
the universe always conspires with you to bring you
to the most optimal outcome of good.
But when you unconsciously continue to accept the bad
that is hurled at you and begin to identify with it every day,
the universe will continue to throw you more bad in the form of lessons
until you finally succeed in burying yourself
beneath a shroud of depression and sadness.

Are you ready to break bad? Your life is waiting to get good.
Let's start transforming it. You will be rewarded every step of the way.

... it always does.

Our life lessons are grouped. *It is rare that you will be dealt just ONE lesson; they usually travel in packs.*
It is best to be prepared for them.

It is also important to realize that you are not being punished and that you are not a victim of them.
You are, in fact, in total control of how you get those lessons (or if you get them at all).

Say you are in an important lesson-learning phase of your life to learn one major lesson (e.g. self-esteem) and you have 10 tests coming up to deliver that lesson to you. Your testing period could last as little as three months or as long as 10 years.
You are in control of how quickly you get that lesson.
Every time you get hit with the lesson, if you can pick yourself up and identify the lesson, then you will have "won" that round.
Then the universe serves up the next test to you to see if you get that one. All the tests support the same lesson so it gets easier to see.
The quicker you get the lesson, the quicker you get dealt the next test and ultimately the quicker you work through all tests.
When you finish the tests, you have truly gotten the lesson and the lesson STOPS.
You are free.

Now, if you choose to NOT get the lesson and just feel sorry for yourself and play the victim, then the universe will hold off dishing you up the next test because it waits for you to be "relatively" ready for it.
In your attempt to be happy, you keep yourself in a space of non-learning which feels like an unhappy, stagnant and frustrating space where nothing new happens.
Maybe you have been there before?

When it rains, it pours. Let it pour down on you. Grow through those tests and get that lesson. Tell the universe to give you its best shot. *If you are smart, you will NOT stay inside to avoid the rain, you will get a great umbrella and learn to dance your way through the rain.* Life continues and the storms will get easier with each lesson learned. Are you ready to get wet?

The Log That Saves You

... will eventually pull you down.

You cannot continue in a pattern of survival forever.
But there is always the tendency to get stuck on that log.
After all, it saved you at one point, and out of habit
it is easy to grow dependent upon it.
But dependency never yields success.
Relying on your log for survival gets old fast and
eventually you tire of holding it,
the log yields to your weight and you both sink.
So what once saved you will ultimately destroy you
if you do not allow yourself to evolve beyond it.

The game is not about surviving but thriving.
You have to learn to move beyond the safety net of
what once served you and push the boundaries into a new life for yourself.
No one is going to do it for you.
Holding onto that log does not keep you safe,
it holds you back from becoming great.

We all have our logs in lives – the people, the jobs, the situations
that came in and saved us at a time when we needed it.
That time is now over and the rest of your life is ready to begin.
Learn to leave those logs behind and trust yourself that you can swim to
a new side of that lake and create a new life for yourself.
Any time you are ready to let go of your log,
the rest of your life is waiting to begin.
Are you ready to take a chance?

When You Are In a Hole

... stop digging.

After all, it's not really going to lift you out of that hole, is it?
A hole takes you deeper.
Once you realize that,
it is easier to make another choice for yourself.

We have a tendency to prove our own undoing.
We dig ourselves into our own emotional holes.
Every time we choose to dwell on negative emotions,
we choose to dig that hole deeper.
Every time we choose to buy into others' criticisms of us,
we dig ourselves deeper even still. In fact,
it is very easy to bury ourselves beneath a shroud of negative emotion,
insecurity and inferiority.

You have a choice every day as to whether you will allow your negative
state of emotions to affect you.
You also have a choice as to whether you will allow
other people's negative state of emotions affect you.
When dealing with others, it is important to remember that
those emotions, criticisms and critiques are not yours, so why own them?
You NEVER need to accept any of that as fodder
to help you dig yourself deeper. It's simply not necessary.

No one is digging that hole for you, but YOU.
If you are in too deep, it is time to throw away the shovel
and climb back out. Decide today that you choose NOT to be buried by
your own or others' negative rhetoric.
You choose happiness and freedom from negative thought.
Your life is yours. At some point, you must come to the conclusion that
you are done beating yourself up. You deserve better.
Once you can see that, the shovel no longer looks attractive.
Trade in your shovel for new soil that will promise
to grow you tomorrow's abundance.

When The Burden Gets Too Heavy

... learn to lighten your load.

Not every issue has direct relevance on your life.
Yet as humans, we tend to carry every burden on our shoulders
as if it were our own. Maybe we are empathetic,
maybe we are sensitive to other's plights, maybe we are just kind people –
whatever the excuse, we do not need to carry others' issues,
struggles or negative behaviors upon our shoulders.
Life gets much simpler and easier when we learn
to own what is ours and give the rest back.

Your work in life is to get yourself to the "top of the mountain"
with as much ease and enjoyment as possible.
You cannot get to the top of the mountain with ease
if you are carrying bags upon bags of other people's traumas
and opinions and judgments.
In order to succeed in your own life,
you have only to carry what you need in order to make yourself happy.
When you have what you need, you have enough to share with others,
but when your bags are full of what isn't serving you,
you take yourself down, exhaust yourself and leave yourself
feeling hopeless and filled with despair.

Decide today that you are not going to hold onto anything in life
that doesn't serve you – whether it may be a certain person or
other's opinions of you, or other's dysfunction with themselves
or with their peers, etc.
Whatever drama or nonsense is going on around you,
learn to let it pass through you.
Don't pack it up and take it up the mountain with you.
If the situation doesn't have a direct bearing on your life
in a POSITIVE WAY, learn to not take it on as yours.
The work in life is in learning to streamline your baggage,
not in carrying everyone else's up the mountain.

Carrying other's burdens does not make you the superhero;
it makes you the fool.
After all, your carrying their baggage doesn't help them learn their lessons,
and by doing so, you have just made life harder for yourself.
Who wins here? No one.

Give your back a rest.
Give others their own baggage to carry up the mountain.
Everyone will get there in their own time and
with their own learnings and comfort level.
Let the journey to the top begin.
Are you ready to take a chance?

The Only Way Out

... is through.

You NEVER overcome your problems by abandoning your path.
You only succeed by seeing it through.

In life it doesn't matter what you are going through;
it only matters that you get yourself through it.
Getting through it teaches you about yourself –
it gives you a new set of tools to learn how to live your life.
And once learned, that set of tools will forever pave the way
to a happier and more fulfilling existence for you.

The truth is that you can never hide from your pain.
It is always there, but you have a choice as to how you can deal with it.
If you succumb to the pain, it will always win,
but if you stand up to it, it will never be able to stop you.

Running from your problems NEVER solves them.
Trying to avoid the pain only delays the inevitable.
The only way to get to the other side is to brave
your way through the lesson, the hardship and the pain.
It may not be the popular response,
but it is the only constructive response.
Once you can move beyond the painful experience,
that experience is free to shift for you and the sun comes out again.

Sitting out on the grass in the pouring rain only gets you wet.
Crying about it will not keep you dry,
but if you get up off the grass and run towards shelter,
you have half a chance of staying dry.
You cannot think your way through your pain,
you have to get up and take action in order for things to change.
The only way out is through.
Are you ready to go through it all to get to the other side?
Your ability to heal is contingent on it.
Are you ready to take a chance?

It's Always Darkest Before The Dawn

... that is how you know a new day is coming.

Just when you think you cannot bear anymore darkness, life shifts.
It has to. *Nothing ever stays the same.*
Life is in constant fluctuation and change.

The ending of a phase of life heralds in the dawn of a new day.
It is important to remember the nature of life's cycles.
Darkness is the phase where one simply cannot see and
light is the phase where answers can be readily found.

When you are in a period of darkness, it can only last so long.
It is NEVER forever. Once it hits its darkest point, the light must return.
Vice versa, once the light has shown us the way,
it is time for the darkness to return
in order for us to learn something new about ourselves.
The darkness brings opportunity for growth.
It brings us situations and people that challenge us and
force us to look beyond our limitations for answers.

The light is our reward for finding our way through the darkness.
The darkness shapes your character and
is one of your greatest teachers.

Don't be afraid of the dark.
Find new ways of moving through the darkness and
keep your head up because you know
once you hit the darkest point, the sun has to return,
it can be no other way. In the interim,
don't just wait for the sun to come out;
learn how to navigate your way through the darkness.
Managing the darkness will make you much happier and
much more adept at enjoying the light of your life.

Turning Stumbling Blocks Into Stepping Stones

... .. is the ONLY way to succeed in life.

You have a choice every day as to whether you will allow yourself
to get tripped up on the stumbling blocks OR
whether you will use them as stepping stones
to a new and better future.

As human beings, it's common behavior to
let the stumbling blocks in our lives take us down and destroy us.
We get caught up in the drama of the stumbling block and forget that
it is our responsibility to get back up and make our lives better
because of what we have experienced.
We sit there for months/years blaming the stumbling block
for throwing us off course. And what does that do for us?
How does that help us or make things better for us? It doesn't.

No stumbling block is in place to make a mess of your life;
it is only in place to help you become stronger, more sound and more stable in yourself.
Stumbling blocks can also be in place to alter your direction in life
when it's time to go down a new road.

Regardless, stumbling blocks are ALWAYS
the impetus for great change and success.
They should never be viewed as obstacles along our path.
Once we learn how to turn those stumbling blocks into stepping stones,
we realize that we can now rise higher then we ever thought possible.
Time to start stumbling!

Conclusion

Here's the deal...

Life is not always going to give you roses, but it is YOUR garden and YOU ARE very much in control of the seeds you plant. So learn to live consciously, be aware of who you are and how you are showing up in life because you will see that the energy you are putting out is exactly what is being mirrored back to you. There should be no surprises when you learn to open your eyes and see your own patterns reflected back to you.

Whether you realize this or not, you are never being punished. You are never the victim of anything that is going on in your life - no matter how bad it is. Everything happens only to bring you to a BETTER place in your life if you can GET THE LESSON and GET OUT. Don't dwell on the lesson and stay stuck in negative cycles over it. Why give your power over to someone or something else to make you feel badly about yourself? It is always a choice. You can either let the lesson take you down or you can take the lesson out. Again, it is always YOUR choice.

Your reactions to the situations in your life are what will determine the next experience you have. If you want to play the victim of your circumstances, you will attract more negativity and negative situations and people into your life. But if you can muster up the energy to pick up and put the pieces back together the best way you know how and keep marching on, the universe will reward you tenfold.

And you do not need to have all the answers. You only need to get up off the ground and take one step, any step in any direction, and then the universe will work with you to bring about the change you desire and deserve. You have free will, so you need to help yourself; no one will do it for you and it is not anyone else's job to do it. But when you can show the initiative to make change, the universe conspires to bring it to you and make it your reality. You are always co-creating your life – each step.

You are dealt life lessons each and every day. By being conscious, you can learn to recognize those lessons and free yourself from the cycle of karmic experience: the cycle of attracting the same lesson over and over again (with different people) until you work it through successfully. Stop repeating the lesson. Once you get it, the lesson stops and you are free to move on to happier pastures. Remember, the longer it takes you to get those lessons, the harder they get.

It all comes down to choices. Your free will gives you the innate ability to choose the direction your life will take. What choice will you make next?

Conclusion

I hope these essays give you some inspiration and help you strategize your next move. If only someone had taught us these simple laws of the universe back in kindergarten, think of how much easier things would have been for us. But you have them now. The rest of your life awaits and it can be handled with much more ease, grace and happiness. What are you waiting for? Best of luck on your journey.

In gratitude,
Donnalynn

Based in New York City, Donnalynn Civello CHHC, AADP is Executive Director of Ethereal Wellness Counseling (www.ethereal-wellness.com) and a Certified Intuitive Life Coach and Holistic Nutritionist and 500hr Yoga Teacher - RYT who is dedicated to helping clients and students find BALANCE in all aspects of their lives - emotionally, mentally and physically.

Certified in Intuitive Counseling and Pranic Healing Psychotherapy, Donnalynn is internationally known for her inspirational insights which are featured on her weekly blog (www.etherealwellnesswordpress.com). She remains dedicated to teaching simple spiritual tools for living your best life. As an Intutive Life Coach, she uses a proprietary methodology to help her clients uncover their *life purpose* and learn their individual *life lessons* so that they can move forward with their lives.

She is an author and motivational speaker and *Stand Up For Passion* advocate (www.standupforpassion.com). She is also a wellness writer and *Yogi Times* Contributing Editor.

Her work has been featured in Glamour Magazine (glamour.com), On Deck with Lucy TV show and Radio Show and on the iHeartRadio Inspirational Network.

For more inspirational thoughts and quotes, you can follow her on:

Twitter – @dlcivello
Instagram - @donnalynncivello
Facebook - @donnalynn.civello
Blog - etherealwellness.wordpress.com

Contact
Website - ethereal-wellness.com
Email - dcivello@ethereal-wellness.com
Office - 419 Park Avenue South; 2nd Floor, NY, NY 10016

CPSIA information can be obtained
at www.ICGtesting.com
Printed in the USA
FSHW011818091019
62852FS